# When the Spirit Moves

## A Guide for Ministers in Transition

**Riley Walker** AND **Marcia Patton**

Foreword by Stephen E. Ott

**JUDSON PRESS**
PUBLISHERS SINCE 1824
VALLEY FORGE, PA

The authors and Judson Press have made every effort to trace the ownership of all quotes. In the event of a question arising from the use of a quote, we regret any error made and will be pleased to make the necessary correction in future printings and editions of this book.

Unless otherwise noted, Bible quotations in this volume are from the New Revised Standard Version (NRSV) copyright © 1989 by the Division of Christian Education of the National Council of the Churches of Christ in the United States of America. Used by permission. All rights reserved.

Scripture quotes marked (NIV) are from HOLY BIBLE: *New International Version*, copyright © 1973, 1978, 1984. Used by permission of Zondervan Bible Publishers.

Interior design by Beth Oberholtzer.
Cover design by Tobias Becker and Bird Box Graphic Design, www.birdboxdesign.com.

Library of Congress Cataloging-in-Publication Data
Walker, Riley.
    When the Spirit moves : a guide for ministers in transition / Riley Walker and Marcia Patton ; foreword by Stephen E. Ott. — 1st ed.
        p.  cm.
    ISBN 978-0-8170-1662-3 (pbk. : alk. paper) 1.  Clergy—Relocation. I. Patton, Marcia. II. Title.
    BV664.W35 2011
    253'.2—dc22
                                                                2011010810
Printed in the U.S.A.

First Edition, 2011.

# Contents

# Foreword

For the new and inexperienced minister, it can be daunting to consider a ministry transition—especially in denominations where policies, expectations, traditional interpretations, and expected standards of performance differ from place to place. Add to this the new minister's relative inexperience in interviewing, negotiating, and advocating for oneself—inexperience shared by many well-meaning church committees—and you can see that often the default method of well-intentioned working together becomes trial and error, with much room for effortful trials and painful errors, hard lessons, misunderstandings, and shortened tenures.

Addressing these issues, Marcia Patton and Riley Walker, each an executive minister of their respective American Baptist regions, have written *When the Spirit Moves: A Guide for Ministers in Transition*. At first glance, it is a book for pastors making a move from one ministry setting to another. But this wise gem of a book is also invaluable for pastoral relations committees, search committees, congregational officers, church treasurers, and laypersons wishing to think more deeply about their pastors' ministries, frustrations, challenges, and issues of excellence in ministry practice.

Covering a wide scope of topics in discussing pastoral calling and the variety of ways one might answer that call, this book offers much in the way of practical guidelines, based in spiritual wisdom and years of experience and reflection. It is plain in speech, and even-handed in its treatment of ministry practice issues. It uses fictionalized vignettes to illustrate teaching points and best practices.

The volume begins with the question of whether to stay or make a move to another ministry setting. The original call to ministry may or may not be all that clear to the minister, and so discernment about a transition can be daunting. The authors suggest that ministers consider what gifts they are able to offer in their present setting and whether there are opportunities to use those gifts as widely as possible. This presupposes that there has been prior reflection and practical understanding of what gifts for ministry the pastor possesses! Do those gifts match the needs of the place of ministry? Do skills need to be added? What is the sense of God's calling? Time and again the authors suggest consulting with ministry colleagues, advisors, mentors, family members, and using the resources of Career Assessment Centers. These Centers are resources to pastors, family members, special ministries persons, missionaries and other church workers throughout the vocational career cycle. The authors remind us that prayer is vital to a grounded discernment process, promoting actively listening to God's response. They write, "Without prayer, without God's participation in our lives in a daily way, all the suggestions ... that follow are nothing. We must put God and concern for God's purpose and people first before we move ahead." (p. 16).

An annual self-evaluation of one's ministry is suggested, both in setting the goals and evaluating the progress made toward attainment of those goals. A spiritual self-evaluation is also recommended, reminding me of the absolutely vital importance of spiritual discipleship and grounding for the pastor.

The authors include wise counsel that an individual's call to ministry can change over time. This is well supported in biblical accounts, but our popular culture sometimes overlooks the fact that *calling* is a verb, and it will transform and change as the one called grows and changes. We should avoid limiting how the Spirit is trying to lead us! Once again, regular review and evaluation help us to be prayerfully purposeful about needed adjustments, performance issues, continuing education priorities, and even family needs. The importance of getting bi-vocational training and developing ministry specialties is mentioned.

A very helpful chapter deals with terminations, both voluntary and involuntary. In it, the authors explore different types of impact on the minister and the minister's family, acknowledging the dislocation and disruptions as well as damage to the trust and acceptance once offered by a congregational community to the new pastor. This chapter includes valuable and practical information about developing an exit agreement and offers a model for such an agreement.

Several chapters deal with the pastoral search and call process, a time in the life of a minister and a congregation that requires clarity around many process decisions and boundary issues. Written agreements about compensation, time off, benefits, parsonage or housing allowance, and continuing education expectations are all discussed. Church search committees, church councils, and treasurers can profit from the information here, and the departing pastor can use the section on transition ethics. The use of denominational resources, consultants, counselors and career centers is once again raised, to work not only with the nuts and bolts of transition but the sometimes intense emotional issues. The appendices are filled with more useful information.

Seminarians should read and be informed by this book, as should those new to ministry and those getting ready to retire. For family members, farsighted church boards and committees, and those who know that change and transition is challenging: there is practical help in these pages. The authors are to be commended for drawing on their years of experience in this book, in order promote excellence in pastoral practice, pastoral retention and nurturance, and healthy church life and habits. With this helpful resource, we are better equipped for service. Out of our hearts may there flow rivers of living water for a thirsty land.

Rev. Stephen Ott, PhD
Executive Director
Center for Career Development and Ministry
Dedham, Massachusetts

# Preface

**M**ost ministers move four to eight times in their career, yet there are few resources to guide them through the search and call process. Most existing materials have been developed to assist churches and search committees. Denominations also focus most of their time and energy on training and supporting churches in seeking the "right one" that God would have serve and lead the congregation. So the question for us emerged: Hasn't anyone been spending any priority time training *clergy* to seek and find the "right" ministry setting in which to serve and lead? That question became the genesis of this book.

Together, we have a combined experience of 40 years in assisting ministers and churches in the search and call process. We are both American Baptist Executive Ministers presently serving fairly small judicatories (what our denomination designates as regions or associations); we have also served as Area Ministers within larger regions. Riley's current region is composed of predominantly rural and suburban congregations, while Marcia oversees an urban region. Marcia also brings years of experience in the intentional mentoring of women in ministry, a perspective that the authors and publisher agreed was critical for this project. Marcia knows from experience that it routinely takes longer for women to find places of ministry, and that moreover, the timeline for placement of women who are not of European heritage is much longer yet.

It is important to acknowledge that we are both Caucasian, and we are aware that the processes presented in this volume are generally true for churches that are predominately Euro-American in heritage. However, we have observed that churches of color (African American, African Caribbean, Native American, Hispanic, Asian North American, and other, so-called immigrant congregations) seem to rely more heavily on the informal network of their church culture in search-and-call efforts than on an established denominational process. For better and worse, this informal networking occurs within most church traditions, but the practice is especially prevalent in non-Anglo churches.

While we come from an American Baptist perspective, we believe we have approached the work of this book so that it might be used by all ministers (especially those within the free-church tradition) as they seek their next call to ministry. Some of the language may be different, but much of the concerns and processes will be the same. We hope that, if you are one of those reading this book because you are seriously considering a ministry move, then you will find these pages helpful.

Often we will talk as though all ministers move from one church ministry to another church ministry. However, we are well aware that this is not always the case. Ministers may move from a church ministry setting to ministry such as chaplaincy, denominational staff, or faith and justice advocacy—or vice versa. Other ministers may move from ministry to secular work or to bivocational ministry. We hope we have included sections that speak to these various needs and concerns, but we especially want to help the minister navigate the terrain of a search process with a local church search committee, a terrain often unknown to both parties.

This book will offer our insights and strategies to assist ministers participate in a more informed manner. For congregational churches, the search and call process has many similarities. Each church system or grouping of churches has a primary method for churches to find ministers and ministers to find their ministry. We will present the expectations and process used by churches to ministers.

Our approach to this work makes the assumption that none of us—clergy, local churches, denominational leaders—is in this alone. We begin with the understanding that God leads and guides us. We proceed in the belief that sensing a call is in itself a discernment process—and that God is in the mix. Part of the question before us is how can we best hear and understand God's purpose for the church and for our individual service. There is no easy answer. Just as God's call was different for Moses and Aaron, for Deborah and Miriam, for Paul and Peter, for Mary called Magdalene and Mary the sister of Martha, for Ephesus and Philippi, for Jerusalem and Samaria, so God's call is different for each individual and situation. What we share in these pages explores a general scope, not a specific map. We hope to identify common areas of concern, common pitfalls and missteps, and common routes to that preferred end, where a minister has found a place of calling that the minister knows is from God and that the ministry setting agrees. It is rarely an easy process, but it can be a fulfilling one. We invite you to join us in discerning when and where the Spirit may move.

# Introduction

Now the word of the LORD came to me saying, "Before I
formed you in the womb I knew you, and before you were
born I consecrated you; I appointed you a prophet to the
nations." Then I said, "Ah, LORD God! Truly I do not know
how to speak, for I am only a boy." But the LORD said to me,
"Do not say, 'I am only a boy'; for you shall go to all to whom
I send you, and you shall speak whatever I command you.
Do not be afraid of them, for I am with you to deliver you,
says the LORD." (Jeremiah 1:4-8)

We often wish for such clarity in being called. God even gives
Jeremiah the words to say! No questions here, no ambiguity, no discernment process needed. Seldom does the process of
receiving a particular call to a particular ministry seem so clearly
articulated in our day. However, God has given us resources and
paths that can help us find our place of ministry, the people for
whom God has given us a word and the community we have been
equipped to lead and serve. The purpose of this book is to identify
those resources that will help ministers find their way along what is
often a confusing and treacherous path.

A call to a particular ministry is initiated by God and confirmed
by the issuance of the call by a congregation or ministry. There are
three parties to this call. In accepting a call the minister accepts an
implied or stated covenant. The congregation or organization that
issues the call also enters into that covenant. Both called minister
and the calling entity are thus responsible to one another and to
God, the third party, for upholding the covenant. This covenant

may end when either minister or ministry becomes convinced that the current season of shared calling has ended. It may also terminate if one or more parties fail to uphold its commitments. One party alone cannot uphold the covenant. For the covenant to be ongoing, both minister and ministry must fulfill their obligations to the call. A part of your discernment in considering a new call is to correctly understand the state of your current call. Have both of you kept your covenant?

As authors, Riley and Marcia want to be clear about the context and extent of our work. Together we affirm that all Christians are called to minister. Some are called to serve as grounds keepers; others are called to serve as classroom teachers in the public schools; others are called to parent children and care for aging parents. We affirm these ministries and many others as vital to the work of God in the world.

In addition to these ministries of the laity, however, the church also has a long tradition of setting apart (ordaining) people called to "professional ministry." And in this book, we will focus on those ministers who are called to some form of professional, ordained ministry. Thus, the general discernment techniques and issues we explore will have particular application in professional ministry settings—both for the called minister and for the calling ministry.

In identifying our audience, we could use the word *clergy* rather than *minister,* but we choose the latter, first, because all who are called to this work should have a sense of it *as ministry,* and second, because while *clergy* may be assumed to serve exclusively as pastors in the local church, *ministers* may be recognized to work in a range of church and parachurch settings.

## Landmarks on the Journey

We start in chapter 1 by asking the question, "Do I stay, or do I go?" We assume here that our readers are already engaged in a professional ministry setting, i.e., one that has financial compensation. Thus, the decision for many ministers is one that requires leaving a setting to which you previously felt called in order to embrace a new season and setting for ministry.

From there we turn to chapter 2, in which the ministry skills of the minister may be evaluated and matched with the current and contemplated ministry settings. What are your gifts in ministries? How have you developed in ministry to this point? What do you sense God equipping or preparing you to do? In addition to assessing your own God-given gifts and skills, it is equally critical you to have tools for evaluating the ministry needs and expectations of their current and future settings.

Chapters 3 and 4 look at some of the more difficult aspects of transition—when a minister is forced out of a placement or when the crossroads of ministry mean evaluating honestly what will be left behind. Ministers need to do this while viewing the realities of family well-being, financial needs, and contextual compatibility. As ministers, we care about the people of God whom we serve, and that may cause doubt or conflict in the discernment process. We hope to help you balance the pain and joy, frustration and love in your current ministry in a way that empowers you to sense the leading of God's spirit.

In chapter 5, we address matters specific to the ministries a minister may be considering—both as a departure point and as a destination. In such assessments, personal history is not necessarily the best guide, because ministers grow and mature with each season of ministry. You are a different person now than you were at your previous search. Thus, in this chapter, we will help you discern which elements of ministry feed or strengthen you and which drain you. (While we will tend to emphasize local church settings, we hope the principles are relevant in considering other ministry placements as well.) Part of discerning where God is leading, is to identify some of the ministerial contexts that God is *not* leading you toward.

Ministers often participate blindly in a search-and-call process that is unfamiliar and foreign to them. Expectations are unclear and rarely communicated by the searching ministry. This is particularly true because organizations continually devise or adapt procedures to more effectively facilitate their own discernment process. How empowering would it be to enter your transition feeling informed and prepared to respond? For that reason, chapters 6, 7, and 8 offer an overview of the typical search process, from the perspective of both candidate and search committee, as well as providing counsel concerning the interview and negotiation of benefits.

Finally, chapters 9 and 10 discuss how to make a ministry transition with integrity. When you come to realize that God is moving you from one ministry to another, things in your ministry will need to change. Faithfulness to God takes a different form during times of transition. Not only will we explore ethics related to decision-making, but we will provide guidelines for leave-taking that are both practical and spiritual. Ministers are led by God's spirit to serve in a particular setting—and then led to serve elsewhere by the same Spirit in a different season. As God's leaders, we are required to remain faithful to that call, even (and especially) while disengaging, searching, and reengaging in another ministry.

Throughout this volume, we endeavor to balance pragmatic concerns and practical decisions with biblical principles and insights for spiritual discernment. For that reason, each chapter concludes with Suggestions for Next Steps *and* Suggestions for Prayer. And it is our prayer that, through this work, you will be equipped in mind and spirit to work through your call and ministry search. Let us begin by considering whether it is time to stay—or go.

> Your word is a lamp to my feet and a light to my path.
> —Psalm 119:105

# CHAPTER 1
# Stay or Go?

"I am going to lay a fleece of wool on the threshing floor: if there is dew on the fleece alone, and it is dry on all the ground, then I shall know that you will deliver Israel by my hand, as you have said." And it was so. When he rose early the next morning and squeezed the fleece, he wrung enough dew from the fleece to fill a bowl with water. (Judges 6:37-38)

*God has called you* to ministry. You know this because people in your church have recognized certain gifts in you and affirmed those gifts and encouraged you to consider parish ministry, or ministry in another setting. You did not come to this place easily or lightly. You came to ministry through prayer. The backbone to all that is said and done in this book is ultimately about prayer that is true communion with God (hearing God speak into your life) and prayer that is contemplative and examining of yourself in relation to God and God's work in the world. Although much of what we say in this book may sound like it is all about you, in reality it is all about God. Without God, any ministry we attempt will be nothing; with God, the seemingly impossible can be possible.

## It Is about Your Call to Ministry

Depending on where you are and where you have come from, the work of deciding what God is calling you to do at a particular time can seem like wandering in the wilderness, with no burning bushes or lights or clouds or angels to lead the way. Transitions in ministry are often the hardest seasons in ministry. The minister considering transition may wish to have Moses' experience— encountering God's direction in the form of a burning bush and clear instructions: Go to Pharaoh and tell him to let my people go. Or you want, like Samuel, to hear your name called in the night and specific words to be put on your lips. Or, even to have a Damascus Road experience like Paul, to have three quiet days to think through your life and get it all figured out by those who come to minister with and to you. Who hasn't wondered, with the power and might of God, why the Spirit doesn't provide a simple itinerary: From this year to this year, serve here, and then go to the next place. But just as your original call to ministry may not have been all that clear-cut, so too the transitional decision of exactly where and when to go can seem daunting.

Whenever we consider ministry as our vocation, we know we do it because God calls us, so in reality God does tell us where to go. However, sometimes the discernment process for what God might have us do becomes murky, or at least it seems so. And our walk with God is a personal and private matter. It is difficult at best to explore this question without putting to the test our foundational relationship with God. The bottom line, though, is that nothing is right if it is not from God, and our first response to staying in one's current ministry or going to a different place is, "What is God telling you?" The second question might be "How is God telling you?" We will attempt to examine some of the ways God might use to tell us the answer to the question, "Go or stay?" We need to remember that God does offer to lead us, and a closer look at some biblical examples will remind us of that fact.

## Called Out of Exile

Moses was a man who had run away from a disastrous experience and was working as a shepherd far from home. One day a bush looked like it was on fire, and a voice came out of the flames claiming to be God. The man believed it was God because he had never seen a bush be in flames but not consumed. In the conversation between the "for the time being" sheepherder and God, God gave instructions to the sheepherder for his next steps in life. The sheepherder was to become a leader of a people.

### A Voice in the Night

There was a young man named Samuel who was serving a well-known minister, doing whatever the minister required him to do. One night the young man was awakened when he heard his name called. He assumed the minister had called his name and went to him to inquire what was needed. However, Samuel was told the minister had not called him. This happened three times. After the third time, the minister realized that it was God who was calling the young man and he should respond to God. When Samuel responded, God told him that he had selected Samuel to be the voice to God's people and gave him specific things to say to them.

### At the Right Place at the Right Time

There was once a woman named Esther who was a queen in the king's palace. The enemies of the Jews had plotted against the Jews. The king needed to be told of the plot, and Esther was the only one with access to the king. Her access was limited and it was dangerous to go forward, but after fasting and praying, she did. It was clear to her and others that she was put in place for just such a time.

## Ministry Where You Are

Having no burning bushes or voices calling in the night, or needs to which it is apparent you are the answer, or even Damascus Road experiences, how does one figure out whether or not one should consider leaving or staying? The dialogue starts with the default of "do ministry where you are."

There is a lot to be said for the attitude that your ministry is where you are. If we see a ministry as a stepping stone to another, bigger place or being where we are as some kind of process to another place, we will not serve the people or God with our whole selves. People who excel in their work do so because their attention and commitment are where they are, not on the possibility of a next place. One minister said that he did not think about what his next position might be or look for another call; instead, he supposed that when he was called to a pastorate, he was called to that pastorate for the rest of his life. Having said that, this good and wise man served four churches before he retired. So, although he entered and remained with this good intention to serve a place for the rest of his life, the only one that worked out as such was his last pastorate. He was there about fifteen years, and he still lives in that community.

If our default is to stay where we are, two questions can be asked that are legitimate: What gifts have I to offer where I am now, and along with that, are my gifts being used in this ministry setting in as many ways as they might be? This second question may help you consider if you need to tweak the ministry where you are to give better satisfaction to yourself and those you serve than to think seriously about moving to another situation. What is being suggested here is that regular evaluation is important during ministry and certainly when considering whether or not to move. If evaluation is done regularly, you will have at hand some measures or notions on which to evaluate when an expected or unexpected offer for a new ministry comes your way.

Some people do yearly evaluations, making careful statements of what they want to achieve in a given year and how they have done in achieving these goals. Others might do something similar but far less formal in nature. The best evaluation is done in conversation with others—a pastoral relations committee, a discernment committee of your own choosing, or a group of trusted colleagues and friends. Evaluation is best done when it is done regularly; annually is recommended. And every five years or so, a more comprehensive evaluation should be done. This is the time when evaluating whether or not your gifts and skills are used to their full potential in the current ministry is legitimate. Every year it is important to ask, "Are the needs of the church or ministry setting being met by my gifts and skills? Is there a skill I need to add to my toolbox? Are there gifts that need to be honed and put to more effective use?" All of these questions can help us not only to determine if staying is the correct answer but also how staying can give us renewed purpose and satisfaction in ministry.

## Why Might I Need to Think about Going?

There are legitimate reasons to decide to seek another ministry setting. On occasion a church or other ministry can make it clear that you are no longer a fit for that ministry. For instance, if the church makes decisions that you can't support, maybe the relationship between the pastor and the congregation has become too broken to repair. Mind you, there is a lot to be said for doing the sacred work of reconciliation, but there are times when it cannot be accomplished. There are times when too much damage can be done to a person or a congregation for the relationship to continue. Caution is in order here, because there are times when leaving is the easy way out, but there are other times when leaving is the right way out as long as it is done the right way (more on this later). An important point about this option is to make sure that you are leaving for the right reasons and that you understand God to be blessing your going. In one of Marcia's pastorates, it became clear at one point that some folk in the church did not understand her ministry. The people were ready to use processes that seemed to her would split the church around her ministry if they were used. She negotiated with the leaders of the church that she would search for a new position. She did not feel at the time that her ministry was complete at the church. In the long run, even though it didn't feel good, it was the right thing to do so the church could move ahead and not get sidetracked.

One important consideration is your family situation. One of the primary gifts God has given us is our family. We believe that God does not place one's family in situations that are unhealthy and unwise for the family. If your spouse needs to live in a particular place in order to find employment, that may make a difference in where you can minister. Or maybe you are responsible for your parents, and that will make a difference about where you can do ministry effectively. Certainly, if your children are a particular age, it may be unwise to think of moving them from one school to another. Notice that we haven't given any particular, hard-and-fast rules on any of these. Because every child is different, every family has different issues and concerns. The one thing we want to be clear about is that the consideration of family well-being is a primary concern.

## How Do You "Figure It Out"?

Everyone has dry seasons, times when it feels that nothing is working well. These pass. But there are also times when it is clear that one's gifts and skills are no longer what the church needs to move forward. This can be a signal that the time has come to go. This is one reason that regular evaluation is a healthy thing. We need wise counsel for these decisions because it is hard most of the time for us to judge our own work and worth. A trusted set of family and friends or colleagues can help make a more reasoned judgment than we often can by ourselves.

### Career Assessment Centers

When considering transition points in life and career, invaluable resources are the numerous centers for career and ministry development. These centers provide objective feedback through testing and interviews. The process is extremely helpful to clergy who are seeking direction in ministry choice, as well as those struggling with work issues or career frustration. This assessment can provide important personal insights for those clergy who are reviewing their professional development or clergy considering new ministry options. It is regrettable that persons wait until they are in crisis to consider this kind of review. By then their options may be more limited and damage may be intensified in the minister and family.

Riley's experience at a center for ministry affirmed that continuing in pastoral ministry was a viable option but further identified skills and interests that would enable him to do judicatory ministry. Previously he had considered only continuing in pastoral ministry by seeking another church to pastor. This insight caused him frame the question, "How can my gifts and skills be used in ministry?" with a broader view. It was an important step to consider options that he had not seriously considered before.

Insightful feedback that career centers provide can be an important affirmation to continue in the same kind of ministry in which you are currently engaged. It may open you to consideration of ministries you are gifted for but hadn't considered. And it can give you permission to exit a ministry for which you are ill-suited. Often your judicatory can assist you with the cost of this assessment. Some judicatories require an evaluation from career assessment centers in preparation for ordination. It is recommended that you return after the first five to ten years of ministry, again at whatever may be mid-career, and finally sometime five years or so before retirement. The feedback offered can be helpful for giving guidance for the next step.

## Discernment Committees

One of the best experiences Marcia had in trying to figure out what was next in her ministry was a discernment committee. She was finishing her PhD (read "working on her dissertation") and had just lost out on getting a job she thought was perfect for her. Her pastor suggested that she gather what he called a discernment committee. Some Quakers use this practice often, he explained. So Marcia asked a small group (about ten to twelve people, as she recalls) of friends, colleagues in her PhD program, church members and, as it turned out, a couple of people who were on the committee that hadn't given her that perfect job! Most people knew each other, but not everyone did.

Marcia recalls that the group had a pleasant time together. They spent about three hours together one evening. The pastor moderated the time. One of Marcia's friends took notes as she shared a little about what she had learned in the last few months of searching for work and what in general she had learned about herself in the process of working on the PhD. She had been working for the PhD to teach in a seminary. The job she had lost out on was a national-level education position for adults, which seemed like a perfect fit. Her doctoral studies were in group dynamics. This discernment group affirmed Marcia's skills and interest. The most useful feedback came in the form of "I can see you doing" applications of her gifts and skills. These persons were able to envision her in ministries that her confidence or humility kept her from considering. The result of the discernment committee was a suggestion to consider ministry at the judicatory level. That surprised Marcia, but it proved to fit her very well. If it were not for that discernment committee, Marcia may have never looked in that direction.

We would recommend a discernment committee as a way of figuring out what might be next for you. We recommend that you get some help in gathering a discernment committee. Ask a trusted friend or colleague or maybe your spouse to moderate; don't try to moderate yourself because it is too hard to hear what is being said *and* moderate the conversation. Keep the group small (six to twelve people). Bring together people who know you from different contexts: friends, colleagues, and ecumenical partners. After prayer (led by the moderator), introduce people in the group, and share relevant parts of your journey that led you to call this meeting. Then ask for feedback. Your moderator may want to stop for prayer after the group listens to your story and certainly at the end of the evening. It is a way for God to speak through others.

Sometimes, because we have made ourselves open to it, God puts a new ministry opportunity in our path that seems to mean that God is saying, "Go!" Again, the caution here is to check that perception with spouse, family, trusted friends, and colleagues. There is a two-part question: (1) Is this a ministry position that calls for my skills and gifts, one that I am ready to at least try? (2) Is now the time to leave where I am? Is it a good time for my family? Is it a good time for my present ministry? Is it good for the congregation I am serving? Those trusted friends, family, and colleagues can help answer those questions in the midst of what may seem like a golden opportunity with wisdom, objectivity, and grace. Don't work in a vacuum. God has given you colleagues and trusted friends who have understanding and insights about you and your ministry.

In the next chapter we will look further at evaluation of ministry and how to assess where you are in relation to where you may consider going. Chapter 4 deals with the situation of pastors who are being forced out of their ministry.

We want to conclude this introductory chapter with the reminder that in all you do to discern where God would have you to serve, prayer is the first, middle, and last thing. Prayer is two-way, not just praying for your wants, needs, and concerns but actively listening to God's response. Without prayer, without God's participation in our lives in a daily way, all the suggestions in this chapter and the ones that follow are nothing. We must put God and concern for God's purpose and people first before we move ahead. With God and an understanding of a call by God to a place, all that is accomplished may surprise people.

## Applying the Principles

Sometimes it helps to paint some pictures. Although some actual situations could be used, we have painted some typical scenes that help to understand better what we're trying to say. While none of these cases are real, they aren't false either; they are composite examples from experience and work. (Because the cases aren't real, the names are fictional.)

### Consistent and Content

Aaron keeps his energy and attention focused on individuals. He enjoys the diversity of ministries he is called on to perform. Worship and preaching are important to him, but so are youth ministry and children's ministry, and he dabbles with a couple of groups who sing for special occasions. He demonstrates consistency of personality and purpose in his pastoral care. Faithfulness to identify needs focuses his ministry. He is careful to remember he is providing a presence of Christ to his congregation. His focus is keeping his flock together and healthy. Aaron doesn't compete with his leaders to maintain the last and strongest voice in church priorities. He values and is empowered by the ministry he does. Aaron feels best suited to serve in this size and type of church.

### From Resistance to Persistence

Katherine was awed to receive a call to a mid-sized congregation immediately after seminary. Her self-employed husband and college-aged children were flexible and supportive, so Katherine dug into the work of ministry. For the first five years things went well, and then hard times hit the community and the church. Membership decreased, and new members were few to none. The church leaders blamed Katherine and began to resist any of her suggestions for change or new programs. Increasingly frustrated and with the support of her ministry advisor and family, Katherine began to look for a new ministry position, somewhere that she could serve God without resistance from God's people. More than a year later, she was still looking and still struggling to serve her current congregation. In time, with support from her ministerial colleagues and husband, Katherine discovered that she had weathered the worst of the storm and found joy in that original ministry. She was glad that God had allowed her to stay, even when everything else seemed to urge her to go.

### Forced Out

A husband and father to three children, Larry was serving happily in his second pastorate. However, after two years, the leaders of the church made it clear to him that things weren't working out. Larry was dismayed and, after lengthy argument, convinced the leaders to consult with the local judicatory. After the meeting, the denominational leader met with Larry. Even though Larry was willing to do anything he could to make things work with the church, his colleague regretfully informed him that the church leaders did not share his commitment. The denominational leader recommended that Larry prepare for a transition to a new ministry. Reluctantly and with his wife's support, Larry updated his résumé, opened his denominational profile, and asked God to go with him and his family in the transition.

### Ministry at the Edge

David was doing well in his church ministry, but he felt his complement of skills was not put to use as fully as he would have liked. His children were grown and out of the house, and he was feeling the need for more of a challenge than parish ministry alone could offer. After years of financial struggle, it would be nice to have a little more income now that he and his wife had more freedom to spend it. After talking with his family, some trusted colleagues, and the local judicatory leader, David decided to leave that church; he was hired by the local school district as a coach and teacher and served a much smaller congregation just outside the city. His bivocational ministry there was more than satisfactory, and he enjoyed that congregation much more than he had the previous one.

## Ministry Stagnation

Gayle has had a good experience in ministry. After seminary she worked as an associate with a seasoned pastor for five years before accepting a call to a small, rural congregation that was delighted to welcome a newlywed pastor with her young husband and infant child. Early in her ministry there, Gayle had twins, and the congregation enjoyed the addition to the church family. The church responded well to Gayle's leadership and made many changes as the years went on. After seven years, however, the church's financial situation was becoming more tenuous. The congregation had stopped growing in membership and attendance, and Gayle was frustrated with the members' apparent satisfaction with the status quo. Maybe it was time for a change. Gayle and her husband agreed that transition now would be better for their family—before the twins started school and their older child entered middle school. After having additional conversations with her spouse, ministerial colleagues, and denominational advisor, Gayle declared her profile open and began to seek a new ministry placement.

## Changing Family Needs

Ezra served as an associate at a great church right out of seminary. He learned a lot from the senior pastor, who soon encouraged him to take a church on his own. Ezra accepted a call to a small church about sixty miles away from the city where his wife worked; they agreed that her commute would be tolerable because they wanted to live in the community with their church members. After two years, however, they had their first child, and their family life changed. The congregation gave their pastor the space Ezra needed to adjust to parenthood, but the commute became increasingly difficult for his wife. For the sake of his growing family, Ezra felt that he must look for a new ministry position in suburban and urban areas where his spouse was likely to find good employment. After discussions with his wife, trusted friends, and denominational colleagues, Ezra opened his denominational profile.

## Suggestions for Your *Next Steps*

- How often are you evaluating your ministry? Monthly, quarterly, annually, randomly, not at all?
- What ministry goals, if any, do you have in common with the congregation?
- Assess your skills and abilities in relation to where you are serving. How well suited are you to your current ministry? What opportunities for growth are present?
- If you are feeling unsettled with where you are currently serving, have you talked with your judicatory representatives? Colleagues? Spouse? Why or why not?
- Consider attending a center for ministry for a career assessment. Visit www.ministrydevelopment.org/centers.html to find an accredited center in your region.
- Consider calling together a discernment committee. Whom would you invite to participate? Why?

## Suggestions for *Prayer*

- In your prayer life, ask God to give you grace and energy for where you are.
- If you are thinking that maybe you need to go somewhere else, ask God to lead you to conversations with family, friends, and colleagues to make it clear.
- Rest in the assurance that God hears our prayers.

# CHAPTER 2

# Matching Ministry Skills and Settings

As Jesus passed along the Sea of Galilee, he saw Simon and his brother Andrew casting a net into the sea—for they were fishermen. And Jesus said to them, "Follow me and I will make you fish for people." And immediately they left their nets and followed him. (Mark 1:16-18)

*When God leads you* to understand that a transition in ministry is right for you, you must give strong consideration to where you *can* go before you consider where *to* go. No minister can successfully go to any ministry; there must be a match between needs of the ministry and the skills of the minister, as well as a call from God. Knowing that God might call you to a new place comes first. What are the signs that God has something new for you? Just as God called fishermen to a life with Christ and bringing the message of hope and peace to people, so God can call forth our gifts for new and different skills.

## Assessing the Skills Needed for Different Ministry Settings

A beginning task is discerning the current best context for your ministry. Because you are a different person with a more matured skill set than you were when you made a previous transition in ministry, you may not want to do and look for what you have done before. You can discern which elements of ministry feed you and which drain you. Family realities can inform you as to what type of community is currently best for you. Part of discerning where you feel God is leading you is to identify some of the ministerial contexts toward which God is not leading you.

As a professional church leader, it is essential that you have a realistic understanding of where your skills and experience have prepared you to serve. Knowing one's gifts and styles, strengths and limitations is one of the best gifts we can give ourselves and others as we search for a new ministry position.

Larry was serving a congregation of about fifty people and having trouble with a couple of strong personalities. He approached a staff person in his judicatory and asked that his name be presented to a nearby congregation that had about three hundred people in worship. Larry did not understand the basic differences between where he had served and the expectations of the church he had expressed interest in. He did good work in a smaller church where he received direction from others. The administrative boards in the church he thought he wanted to go to were larger than the church he was serving. He wasn't prepared to spread his attention this widely. With multiple conflicting expectations, he would have been paralyzed. Knowing our limitations and strengths helps us be realistic about our possibilities and ultimately will help us be called to a new place that will allow us and the people we serve to thrive.

Ministers can assess best context for ministry with honest assessment from themselves and others. If you are honest with yourself, you will seriously listen to others with the gifts of wisdom and discernment. We encourage you to look at the broad strokes of your ministry and not at individuals or specific situations. Working with a particular person may be positive or negative, while how you react to a specific situation may help you know yourself to a certain degree. It is wise to look at the whole, at what energizes you and at what drains you, for this process will help you in figuring out what might be helpful to have in your next place of service.

The importance of various criteria will vary from one minister to another; this chapter will explore the most visible issues. Once we understand the differences in significant aspects of church life we are ready to ask, "Where can my gifts and interest take me?" These same kinds of considerations can be established for non-church-based service or ministry.

Patricia M. Y. Chang's research indicates that 14 percent of first job positions for ordained clergy are secular. At the seventh position, secular employment has risen to 29 percent.[1] There are as many reasons for the vocational change as there are clergy making the choice. The vulnerability caused by being in a high-visibility lifestyle does not work for many people. The door from church-based ministry to secular employment is not a one-way exit. Many clergy move in and out of church-based employment. Clergy can be geographically anchored by the employment of a spouse. If they feel it is time to leave their current church and another isn't available, they move to secular employment for a time.

Dean R. Hoge and Jacqueline E. Wenger were commissioned by the Pulpit and Pew Project at Duke Divinity School to gather data on why ministers leave local church ministry. Their primary conclusions were that young ministers become frustrated, feeling they can't significantly affect the church they are serving. The other reasons can be restated to say that the reward is less than the personal investment. This is often concurrent with feelings of a lack of denominational support.[2]

## Your Origin May Determine Your Destination

Our experience with our church of origin, church experiences prior to ministry, and churches we serve in ministry bias our understanding of church life. The pastor who grew up going to church with his family is going to approach ministry differently from the woman who came to know Christ through justice and advocacy work. Her experience will differ from that of the man who came to Jesus when he was in the army, and his experience will be different from that of the woman who met Christ while in college. Our first experiences of church and our formative experiences of church life will mean a lot about how we view and understand how church should be done. Attending seminary or Bible college will also make a difference. The more we understand our roots and culture, the more we will be able to find the right context for our ministry and connect with the people we work with in a local church.

Someone who grew up in a relatively large church (four hundred people in attendance on Sunday morning) may find that working in a small congregation (fifty people in attendance on Sunday morning) feels awkward and unfulfilling. The opposite can also be true. People who grew up in a small neighborhood church may find that they do not know what to do in a much larger congregation because they don't know how that system works. Our experience can prepare us for a certain type of ministry. An examination of our cultural experience in the church can help us as we seek to analyze what kind of position might suit us in the long run. These life experiences influence our ministry and what we do in ministry.

## Congregational Size Is the Primary Determinant of Skills Needed

This section is not about churches and how they differ by size. It is about you and consideration of your being able to serve a particular church. Each congregation is shaped by being rural, urban, or in a town. Socioeconomic factors cause a congregation to engage in the community around it or to isolate itself. A church's self-image is its perception of the sum of its experiences. Remember to take a macro view of the church in your considerations.

God has raised up congregations of all shapes and sizes. Each manifestation of the Body of Christ is valued and loved by God. It is our conviction that God will prepare and call ministers to serve in all of these contexts. Congregations that are small, single-celled bodies are not lesser before God. Similarly, large, complex organizations are not the divinely intended state for each congregation. A very small percentage of ministers progress upwardly through the sizes and types of congregations. God prepares and calls ministers to serve churches as they are. Often ministers are gifted by the Holy Spirit to serve a specific size or culture of congregation. Finding the place where God uses you and blesses you is the goal. Bigger is not always better.

Congregational size is the most influential shaping factor in the skills and abilities a pastor needs. Congregational size largely defines the minister's responsibilities and authorities. Smaller congregations assign broader personal responsibility and little authority to ministers. Larger and more complex systems invest more authority and oversight to the minister. It is essential to success and survival that we know what the congregation expects our role to be.

Church size is a shaping reality because of relationship dynamics, not only because of a numeric value. In larger contexts, most relationships are at an acquaintance level. This will change the level of trust that leaders are granted. Smaller churches act as a committee of the whole, a fact that gives everyone equal information and input. The size of the congregation dictates the nature of the relationship that "nonleader" members have with the pastor. In large congregations, the pastor may have direct contact only in special circumstances.

Church size is a useful tool for understanding the visible and hidden dynamics of a church. Large churches grant authority to ministry teams and committees. Smaller churches tend to hold a tighter control, requiring those with responsibility to come back for instructions and permission.

An essential piece of stewardship of our call to ministry is skill building. We need to use and grow all of the gifts that God has given us. This is important within the context of our current ministry and in the context of being prepared for where we are called to serve in the future. We want to state clearly that we believe that only a small percentage of persons called to ministry will serve a large church as pastor. The skill sets we present do not imply a successive process for all ministers. Professional church leaders tend to serve most of their ministry in a group of similar-type churches.

The experience in ministry that we accumulate should raise our expectation of our self. You need to be aware that different churches as well as different size and style churches demand an expanding skill set. Have you developed a package of skills to use in your future ministries?

# Church Types

## Family Church

The family church as presented by Arlin J. Rothauge is composed of from 0 to 50 active members.[3] The structure of the family church is a single-cell unit. This is primarily a nuclear family plus extended family members. In other circumstances the single cell may be united by another context. Riley has worked with one family church, which was typical in every other sense than being related. They were formed in a new church start; all are leader types and have functioned as a cohesive unit for more than twenty-five years.

In the life of a family church, the pastor or spiritual leader will function as chaplain but not as the primary leader. Responsibility is assigned to the pastor but no authority. The actual leaders, patriarchs and matriarchs who may or may not be in elected positions, hold authority and make decisions. The pastor is not granted decision-making power and often doesn't even have input. This size system can have congregational polity, but real decision making occurs outside the church meeting. Leadership is not solicited from the pastor or honored. Marry us, bury us, come when we are sick, and otherwise wait until you are called for—these are the unwritten and often unspoken rules. If we as clergy can't accept this reality or try to assume another role, ministry is spent in frustration and in conflict. A mutual ministry and cooperation can be achieved when participants play their assigned roles. This harmony can give rich rewards of familial support and a profound sense of belonging.

As clergy considering a church this size, do not be misled by verbiage expressing a desire for growth and change. Churches are what they intend to be. For a family church to grow, its organization and leadership structure must be transformed to a structure that will allow shared governance and shared vision.

Before discussing skill sets needed for various congregations, it is useful to acknowledge that the following core skills are somewhat cumulative. They do not cast an unbearable burden on clergy to accumulate them like merit badges. Because the ministry required in different-size churches is so different, one never has to apply all of these skills equally. The pastor of a corporation church does not do much visitation in nursing homes but still needs a caring nature. A minister of a pastoral church needs to share ministry responsibilities with lay persons, but not to the extent that a minister in a program church needs to share with staff persons in a team ministry.

## CORE MINISTRY SKILLS AND PASTORAL SKILLS

Preaching                        Caring, Nurturing

Christian Education               Relationship Building

  Programming                  Faithfulness

Youth Ministry                   Consistency

Music Ministry                   Presence

Children's Ministry

Preaching is not of stand-alone importance, but it is often the most visible and thus the most exposed skill. Preaching has two primary components: preparation and delivery. The family church will allow significant time to develop both components. With experience, preparation becomes more efficient. With intentionality, sermon delivery becomes more effective. If a first pastorate is in a family-size church, this is a time we can find our voice for preaching.

A caring and nurturing nature makes us approachable. As clergy we must be able to set our self, our needs, and our views aside to give full, caring attention to another. Listening is one of the purest forms of caring, and too often we fog the event with our opinions and solutions, when what the person is asking for is a caring, safe environment in which to express himself or herself. Nurturing is a context-appropriate empowerment of the person or group we are dealing with. It is a calling of the group or individual to full edification of their abilities.

Relationship building and sustaining is essential. It is not possible to create a meaningful relationship with every person in our ministry, but we bear the professional responsibility to offer that to each person. The best we can do is offer the person space but stay in relationships enough to offer ministry. Some persons or groups will respond positively, and some will not, but it is necessary that we offer the best of our self to each situation. If realities beyond our control won't allow a positive relationship, everyone will be better off if we seek not to feed damaging interactions. In each ministry we will be presented with persons with whom we can create wonderful relationships. We will have some folks we don't like and some folks who don't like us. There will also always be a large group of acquaintances who prefer a relationship with self-defined distances. Developing your emotional intelligence to build healthy relationships across the relationship spectrum is worth the time and effort.

Congregants need a dependable faithfulness and a degree of transparency from us. While we have good days and bad, we must manifest our faith and even the struggle of faith to those we serve. What is called for is a life consistent in faith, not a false face of faith.

Consistency is a reasonable expectation of our selves. We should not give away our faith for indulgences of anger, habit, or hobby. Pastoral presence is a skill, too. Having good listening skills and the personal maturity to comfort with silence practices best pastoral presence. We must have the ability to be with and minister to a diversity of persons experiencing a diversity of emotions. We need to be able to set aside our needs for the time to convey compassion and empathy appropriate to what our congregants are experiencing.

### The Pastoral Church

The pastoral church is composed of from 50 to 150 active members and is made up of two to three cells formed by strong relationships. These cells may be formal: for instance, the women's organization or choir. They may be more informal, such as the group of parents who are teachers or caregivers for children. A group of parents with children the same age can function as one of the relationship groups. This may manifest a mixture of unifying sources, family groups, interest groups like choirs, common profession, or shared life experience. In Riley's first church the Sunday school class for senior citizens was named the Victory class. It originated during the Second World War as a young couples' class and had stayed together for forty years.

Because the cells arise from differing sources they each need a voice in leadership. Each cell sends leaders into a leadership circle. The leadership circle replaces the singular leadership role of patriarchs and matriarchs, because relational units need to select a leader. While the long-time members and prominent persons are present and high-functioning, none of them carries all the role and authority of the matriarchs and patriarchs.

A new structure of representative leaders is formed around a pastoral care center. This religious personage (i.e., the pastor) is usually a paid professional with credentials of higher education. He or she is an agreed-upon religious functionary whose presence is necessary to validate gatherings and activities as legitimate parts of church life. Thus this pastor has to attend or be present for the activity or gathering to be real church. It is a ministry first of presence. Because presence rather than function is the primary role, some authority, but not much, is vested in the pastor of a pastoral church.

As trust is built, the pastor can become a player-coach but won't be allowed to just coach. The members look first to the pastor for direction, inspiration, and pastoral care. Second, they expect the pastor to do the religious work of communion, baptism, preaching, and visiting the sick. The effectiveness of the leadership circle and pastor will depend largely on good communication with the congregation and the ability of the central leader to delegate authority, assign responsibility, and recognize the accomplishments of others. Without such skills, the central pastoral function weakens the entire structure. The leadership required of the pastor is predominantly pastoral because there are so many relationships to watch over in this very large family. Good conflict management skills are necessary for survival, because the pastor is not allowed to become a major power player.

## CORE MINISTRY SKILLS + PASTORAL CHURCH SKILLS

| | |
|---|---|
| Communication | Stress Management |
| Administrative Skills | Organization |
| Multiple Power Foci | Follow-through |
| Multitasking | Leadership Skill |

Every ministry setting requires strong communication—but different settings require different types of communication strengths. A small setting usually assumes a lot of face-to-face, one-on-one inter-action. A context of medium complexity expects that the minister communicate with leaders and with boards. Larger contexts will rely on mass communication either from the pulpit or the website or print newsletters. Pastoral counseling demands more specialized communication and listening skills. Hospital chaplaincy may require presence and reassuring body language (nonverbal communication).

When we serve a midsized church, we need to have our communication skills broadened. We need to be able to communicate effectively in our preaching, in leading worship, in small groups and interpersonally. We also need to have honed our written communication skills. People will remember what they thought we said, so we need to develop as much clarity and intentionality as possible.

It is not possible to eliminate stress in life or ministry. Understanding what our major stressors are is as important as learning to manage them. Ministry has multiple demands with seemingly every changing expectation. Often it occurs at significant levels of intimacy. We must learn to meet our own needs apart from ministry. It is good stewardship to make yourself and your health a priority.[4]

We must assist the congregation with planning and then follow through. We must enable the congregation to set priorities and execute decisions. As an individual, you must demonstrate the personal integrity of follow through. Administrative skills include being able to see the jobs that need to be done, organizing them, finding folks to carry them out, trusting them to complete the task, and following up to celebrate a job well done.

A complicating reality in the midsize congregation is the appearance of multiple power foci: multiple groups and persons vie for time and resources within the congregation. One of our primary responsibilities when working with these competing elements is communication and coordination. We are often the only person attending all of the meetings. It will be necessary to communicate priorities and plans from group to group. While serving this size church, we will be called on to exercise leadership. We need to act as a catalyst to take things from agreed-upon idea to action. It is not enough to be an idea generator; we must facilitate planning, staffing, and resourcing ideas toward their implementation. Leadership skills can be innate or learned, but they must be present. It is necessary to know how to take something from idea to implementation, then to evaluation and adjustment.[5]

## The Program Church

The program church has 150 to 350 active members and is usually in a larger town, urban context, or growing suburb. The maxim "Find a hurt and heal it" characterizes the ministry drivers of many program churches. The ministries will be diverse, unique, or common, and they will be held together by a common unifying vision. Because of the increased size of the program church, authority is delegated with responsibility. The central leader will have a priestly role and will no longer be able to maintain pastoral contact with the whole congregation. Ministry teams will implement the various ministries. The church staff and key lay leaders will provide training and empowerment. The central pastor will serve as pastor, primarily to the church staff and key lay leaders. Currently there is an emerging leadership model that moves away from democratic organization and toward a select leader group who hold closely the unifying vision or purpose.

Leadership by the laity is the key to effective ministry in the program church. The pastor and church staff delegate more responsibility and authority to the laity. Team leadership will replace centralized leadership for ministry planning, coordinating activities in the life of the church, and implementation of ministry. Meaningful ties need to be cultivated and maintained to keep strong ministry leaders from drifting into personal ownership of a ministry or conflict with the direction of the church as a whole. The church staff and lay leaders will require more training and pastoral support for their expanded ministry.

The central pastor becomes a pastor to the lay pastors. The program church is a group of small "congregations" sharing personnel, facilities, and vision. The central pastor is focused on calling the church to live out its calling. Coordination and resourcing become the lifeblood of a healthy church as the parish life centers on separate programs and worship services. Unity and function become the primary tensions. Communication builds bridges of trust. A significant risk is that centrifugal force from the diverse ministries might become a stronger force that the unifying vision.

Each church size offers varying ministry paradigms. Clergy must be able to meet the system needs of a particular paradigm. The pastoral church offers clergy a narrower range of ministry and freedom from the responsibility of managing and guiding the system. The pastoral church increases the range of ministry expectations and slightly increases the input of the clergy. The program church tends to remove the clergy from broad personal contact and captures them behind the bright lights of visibility and accountability.

### CORE MINISTRY AND PASTORAL SKILLS +
### PROGRAM MINISTRY SKILLS

| | |
|---|---|
| Cast Vision | Trust |
| Use Process | Accountability |
| Time Management | Ability to Work through Others |
| Shared Ministry | |

Churches need a unifying vision that is articulated and championed by the lead pastor. A vision at its best is captured from the congregation and matured by ministry. Congregational ownership of vision rises from the values of the congregation and the minister. It is necessary to rehearse the vision to solidify it.

A ministry with a more limited scope will require much more in-depth development in specific skill sets. However, one will need to be effective in what we define as basic ministry skills: caring, nurturing, relationship skills, faithfulness, consistency, and pastoral presence. Whatever the specific scope of our ministry, it is best done from a posture as one called to serve and lead God's people.

Part of leadership in the program church setting is being able to work beyond your own fingertips. The ability to share ministry is a necessity. This sharing requires personal confidence on the part of the senior minister; it requires trust in colleagues. We must learn to be comfortable with letting things go. Leaders can do this by focusing on what, not how. When we agree on what, the how is up to the implementer. As head of staff, Riley tells colleagues, "Once or twice a year I will say it has to be my way; the rest of the time it's up to you."

A need to control can impair our ability to work with and through other staff and laity. If we have low self-esteem, we will hold on to control because we fear the loss of self-worth. We may be manifesting control to avoid emotional pain. Fear of failure or loss will also cause us not to relinquish control. We need a strong sense of self-worth and a willingness to face pain and failure to work effectively with others. Compensating and smiling won't lessen your inner turmoil. We must identify and face our fears to function successfully in this more visible ministry role.

A necessary part of leadership is knowing how to work in a system. In the program church, there are many stakeholders who need to be some part of the process. Investing in the internal church process will increase not only quality but also ownership.

Time management becomes necessary in the program church, because the job can't be finished by 5:00 p.m. on Friday. We must manage our time well because ministry is interruptions: interruptions of funerals, illness, personal crisis, and community crisis. Effective ministers must know what can wait until next week and what has to be done now. The professional aspect of ministry demands that we work until we have our task done. This gift earns us the freedom to control our own schedule.

### The Corporation Church

This congregation has 300 to 500 or more active members. A corporation church has more complexity and diversity; it contains many characteristics from the other church configurations but in a more extreme fashion. The head pastor is a symbol of unity and stability in a system filled with winds of advocacy. The system is multilayered and diverse. The pastor empowers professional staff and a multilevel lay leadership. The system is too large and too complicated for the head pastor to touch all segments of the system. The corporation church is a set of family churches, pastoral churches, and program churches that meet together to share leadership, resources, and facilities. There can easily be twenty fellowship or ministry units that are a person's primary relationship in a corporation church. These units include choirs, accountability groups, recreation groups, young mothers' groups, senior citizens' groups, Bible study groups, and intercessory prayer groups. Social interaction patterns don't allow us to relate to four hundred people. We have a group of five or so friends and fewer than fifty acquaintances. A larger social cluster is a combination of smaller, more cohesive groups.

While maintaining a pastoral mindset and performing limited pastoral activities, the pastor is leader, shaper, and in many ways the face of the ministry. "Catalyst" is a working description of the leadership and role of the pastor. A minister who can do self-assessment rather than self-judgment has the beginning skills for effective self-development. A keenly honed leader has an understanding and acceptance of the scope of his or her leadership.

## CORE MINISTRY, PASTORAL, AND PROGRAM MINISTRY SKILLS + CORPORATION CHURCH SKILLS

Willingness to Engage Conflict   Personal Resilience
Decision Making   Spiritual Maturity
Collaboration

Large congregations will be filled with multiple ideas competing for priority. It is important that clergy be able to manage dissonance at many levels of intensity. The clergy also must have the insight and skills to deescalate these competitions when possible.

Decision making will be expected of the lead pastor of this church. Specific sets of responsibility and authority will leave many decisions to be made by the pastor. Collaboration skills are also required, but after all the considerations, the pastor will need to decide. Spiritual maturity and emotional maturity are both required because the increase in responsibility puts more stress on the lead pastor. There is nowhere to run and hide from the pressure. We must have appropriate coping skills, but the pressure must draw the best out of us.

This church will also require personal resilience. The constant demands and pressures will take a considerable toll. Ministry at this size congregation requires self-regeneration by the ministers. A strong support system is needed because we can't call time out. Without this personal resilience, we are much more vulnerable to unhealthy acting out.

The increased size of the congregation requires the pastor to call and maintain very gifted ministers for the staff. These ministers must have coaching and teaching skills. Assessment and discernment become increasingly important in the pastoral role. The required skill set is a selective utilization of all the identified skills required by other church sizes. The greater the size of the congregation, the more intentional effort will be required for each focused ministry. Staff, influential lay leaders, and implementers will need to leverage adoption and implementation.[6]

## Additional Factors That Shape the Role of Ministry

When one compares the relative size of the church with the role of the pastor, the influence of the pastor increases with the size of the church. For the lead pastor, the range of tasks reduces as the size of the church increases. Conversely, the smaller the church, the less influence the pastor has and the broader the range of tasks. A pastor needs many years' tenure to change these realities. This is a structural reality, not a function of skill or personality. The smaller family church holds the power and unofficially delegates responsibility to respected persons. Most often these are persons who have maintained participation and voice. They are often leaders of their generation in church life. They gain credibility by being seen as spiritual persons.

In the pastoral church, the pastor has influence rather than direct power, so the minister will rely on building relational capital to communicate vision and effect change. In the larger program church, the lead pastor has vested authority, including the power to hire and fire staff without congregational input. However, that minister must be willing to trust those to whom he or she delegates—and to accept a personal role that is more removed from the average member and more limited in the range of ministry tasks. Within the corporation church system, there are stronger internal competing dynamics. Specific ministries will have more ownership and advocacy. The congregation will encompass greater diversity. And the competition for priority and resources will demand that the pastor be willing to engage in conflict. Typically there are also more leaders engaged in the work—ideally leaders who are connected to the parishioners and trusted by the pastor. Don't forget where you are and what the real rules are.

Churches can inflate these ranges within certain limits. But this inflation is not permanent until and unless the system has transformed its structure and power dynamics. Almost any system stumble or upset will bring about a contraction to the churches' historical ranges.

We have identified which skills, in our judgment, need to be present and actualized to serve congregations of varying sizes. However, many of these skills are global and need to be a constant part of any pastor's or minister's skill set. For instance, the need for skills in managing stress and realistic self-understanding are needed life skills, not just ministry skills.

While Rothauge's insight is valuable, no single insight can hold the entirety of Christ's church. Israel Galindo contends that size alone is not a stand-alone determinant, but that churches in the family and pastoral groupings manifest internal forces that determine the boundaries of the parish.[7] Relationship dynamics can make churches essentially a closed system. Entry and participation are hindered by a sense of them and us.

If a congregation has an exclusive sense of self, that perspective will cause them to expect ministry to be focused on the existing group. The role of the minister is to serve the needs of the already gathered flock. Encourage and nurture us; don't challenge our norms.

Congregations of several sizes can manifest the same leadership patterns that smaller churches do. In the larger version there can be two or three extended families that consistently set the norms for congregational life. Sometimes there are larger congregations with shepherding expectations of ministry: "Keep us together as we move through life; we don't need leadership." In such contexts, ministry is done out of personal relationships.[10]

It is essential that we as clergy have a realistic understanding of our spiritual gifts and ministry skills. There is strong need to have this understanding of our strengths so that we can interface with the giftedness of congregation members. Where we are the sole minister, we need to help shape the ministry expectations toward things that we do well. In situations where there is multiple staff, we need to know what to delegate and what to keep. Gift assessment is a meaningful part of our trusting God to provide spiritual gifts to meet the ministry needs where we serve. We may not understand the significance of skill accumulation until ministry needs demand them in our current or future ministry.

## Applying the Principles

### What Kind of Church?

Aaron's wife, Karen, got her dream job, which made relocation to another state necessary. It was complicated, but Aaron stayed in his church and his wife moved to their new city. Aaron had his résumé circulated and felt fortunate that several churches of varying sizes were seeking a minister. The Mount Carmel church contacted him, and he was excited; it was about eighty attendees larger than his current congregation. This church also had two part-time staff persons and a full-time secretary. As he prayerfully considered this context, Aaron was not able to envision himself supervising a staff. After that, he focused on congregations that were of the size and structure he was currently serving. He felt he could offer the church more when he was using gifts and skills that were proven. Aaron liked ministry focused on persons. He was doing a good job and was being energized by the ministry.

### This Works for Me

Ezra is in his second church. He enjoys creating the whole worship event and regularly involves others in the services. He is realizing that he functions best when he knows what is going on in the whole life of the church. It is important to him that the multiple church boards maintain good communication with each other and with the church. Ezra has a strong commitment to expanding the ministry footprint of the congregation and to growing the congregation. He does a good job of keeping up with the ministries in all segments of the church and is present when those segments have events. Ezra's demonstrated skill set is a good fit for a church with a worship attendance of 110. He likes that he has a role in the ministries and that he has a voice in leadership. He describes himself as a player/coach. His church has multiple affinity circles, and each segment has voice in the leadership arena. The church Ezra serves is near a military base, and so much of the congregation changes every three years or so. After much prayer and reflection, Ezra decided that he was best suited to staying where he was in ministry and helping this congregation become the best it could be, to managing its programs well, and to continuing to add people to the church as people are called to different places. He finds that the church is well served by this kind of constant presence.

## A Good Fit

Katherine has a strong skill set from which to minister. She has developed worship skills that demonstrate quality of preparation and polished presentation. She can work effectively one on one, and she enjoys working with groups and ministry teams. Her gifts allow her work effectively with in a complex board and leadership context. Funerals and weddings have become important interactions with the congregation. She communicates well personally and through mass media. She is empowered sharing ministry with others, discovering the group's passions, and casting a vision to the congregation. It is important to her that persons be empowered to minister beyond her presence and planning. Helping persons find their ministry provides great joy. While serving as an associate in a similar size congregation, Katherine found that a church of 150 to 350 provides the resources and challenges that meet her needs. She loves the personal relationships and the more complex corporate aspects of her ministry.

### Growing in Place

Charles was about eight years into ministry. He began to feel it was time for him to go back to school. He knew this next degree would benefit him in his current ministry because he had chosen a program that allowed the students to focus their projects on local ministry priorities. He felt that getting a doctorate would not open any doors for him, but it would at least keep doors from closing. Some of his friends were able to teach in local colleges, and he thought that would be stimulating. He chose to do his course work as distance learning.

When he approached the congregation about doing doctoral work, they were supportive, but a background discussion began about whether or not he would leave as soon as he finished the degree. Remembering what a colleague had done, he offered to stay three years after he finished his degree if the church would pay for one half of the cost. This turned out to be calming; both he and the congregation could see a period of stability before them.

Each one should use whatever gift he or she has received to serve others, faithfully administering God's grace in its various forms (1 Peter 4:10, NIV).

## Suggestions for Your *Next Steps*

- What are your skills in ministry?
- What skills do you have that fit the ministry needs where you are?
- What skills do you need to develop to do a better job or to move to different place?
- Assess yourself in your current context. Are your skills a match for where you are, or are you feeling less than adequate, or are your skills demanding more challenges?

• Do you feel that such self-assessment of your skills is adequate? If not, consider going to a center for ministry or asking respected ministry colleagues to help you take a hard look at your skills.

## Suggestions for *Prayer*

• Ask God to help you make an honest assessment of your skills and abilities.

• Ask God to help you see your worth where you are.

• Ask God to give you vision for your ministry (seeing both where you are and where you might go).

• List insights at the end of each day by the things that delight you and the things that frustrate you as you go about your day.

• Thank God for the delights and ask God's help and insights for the frustrations.

**NOTES**

1. Patricia M. Y. Chang, *Factors Shaping Clergy Careers*, Pulpit & Pew (Durham, NC: Duke Divinity School, 2005), 13–15.

2. Dean R. Hoge and Jacqueline E. Wenger, *Pastors in Transition* (Grand Rapids: Eerdmans, 2005), 36.

3. Descriptions of the different sizes of churches are based on the work of Arlin J. Rothauge, *Sizing Up a Congregation* (New York: The Episcopal Church Center, 1986), 3–5, 10–12, 17–19.

4. Ron Sisk, *The Competent Pastor* (Herndon, VA: The Alban Institute, 2005), 80–81.

5. Sisk, 42–45.

6. Susan Beaumont, "Core Competencies of Large Church Leadership," *Congregations* 35, no. 1 (winter 2009), http://www.alban.org/conversation.aspx?id_7022 (accessed March 29, 2011).

7. Israel Galindo, *The Hidden Lives of Congregations* (Herndon, VA: The Alban Institute, 2004), 78–81.

# CHAPTER 3
# Crossroads in Ministry

"For many are called, but few are chosen."
(Matthew 22:14)

*Every once in a while* we come to the time when we face a crossroads, where going forward where we are is not practical or in more extreme cases where the ministry has said to us, "You are finished here." Sometimes it seems that the first ministry we felt called to, most often the local church, is not where we sense God would have us be at this point. All of this is at the intuitive level. We all come to this crossroads. We question whether we have chosen correctly to serve the local church. Should we seek some other context in which we can serve our calling? Is the ministry we have chosen worth the trouble?

It is a hard and unfortunate reality that there is no guaranteed employment in congregational churches, as there is in some connectional systems. One's call to ministry is essentially a call to sharing the gospel message of grace and mercy. The form of that call will change over time. As professionals, we need to be able to do a fearless inventory of our skills and performance. Are we capable of ministering effectively in our current context? Assessing our ministry is not an easy task, particularly if we have to face the issues involved in not being effective.

If our default is to stay where we are, a legitimate question can be asked: "What gifts have I to offer where I am now?" Along with that, "Are my gifts being used in this ministry setting in as many ways as they might be?" This second question may help you to consider if you need to tweak the ministry where you are to give better satisfaction to yourself and those you serve than to think seriously about moving to another pasture or pastorate.

## Evaluating Your Ministry Skills

It is essential that we as professional church leaders have a realistic understanding of where our skills and experience have prepared us to serve. This self-understanding is a growing awareness. A natural starting place for evaluating your skills for ministry is your experience. What have you done in ministry that you have enjoyed and have received positive feedback from? It is no accident that we wind up in ministries for which we seem to have natural gifts and affinity. God as the giver of spiritual gifts also leads us to utilize these gifts. Service experiences that cause us to struggle and make us uncomfortable also inform us of our gifts and skills. Those ministries that chafe us may not call upon our strengths. And we should avoid including those tasks as significant expectations of our ministry.

Honest feedback from trusted friends and supervisors is informative regarding our giftedness and our function in specific areas. It will be useful for you to expose yourself to many areas of ministry. You will likely be surprised at what you enjoy and what gives you little satisfaction. It seems that one's skill set can shift over time. In specific ministries, known gifts and latent gifts can predominate.

One way to help you articulate your current gift set is to examine a general list of ministry gifts. From a list of items that relate to the life and work of ministry, identify the key areas you feel God is leading you to utilize at this time. Don't be surprised when you see that your gift mix has changed. Gifts that were present but not exercised will move forward as you and your ministry change. Gifts that were not previously affirmed are often present. If there are ministry gifts given by God, it is reasonable to assume that you exercise these gifts in your current ministry or will exercise them in an upcoming context (see Appendix A).

What skills are natural for you? How can you improve those skills? What skills do you need to add to your toolbox? How can you gain experience in that area? A United Methodist resource (see Appendix D) lists twelve functions of ministry and nine personal qualities of ministry. It has been used in the United Methodist system as a way for churches and pastors to evaluate the ministry of the pastor.

It is important to rely on your call to ministry rather than understanding your call to a specific form of ministry. The God who has called you may refocus that call into another context. Do not limit your service by limiting your willingness to consider new options.

Some gifts and skills, such as musical performance, require significant practice and rehearsal. Other skills, such as group leadership, are often intuitive. It is important to remember that your intuitive skills can be honed and enhanced by training and coaching, just as other skills are enhanced by practice.

Your understanding of personal ministry skills and your interest are good indicators but not final determinants of the kind of ministry you are being called to. Local church ministries as solo or senior pastor are not the only viable options. Many persons are gifted and called to ministry in specific areas in the local church. The list of specialized ministries is as broad as the ministry needs of the congregants. Discipleship, youth ministry, children's ministry, pastoral counseling, family ministries, administration, and outreach are common. Additionally, persons may serve as sports and wellness directors, visitation ministers, assimilation ministers, or preschool directors. These persons may or may not experience a shift in their focus of ministry. Not every road leads persons who are called to ministry to pastor a local church, nor should it.

Some people do regular yearly evaluations, making careful statements of what they want to achieve in a given year and assessing how they have done in achieving these goals. Others might do something similar but far less formal in nature. The best evaluation is done in conversation with others—a pastoral relations committee, a discernment committee of your own choosing, or a group of trusted colleagues and friends. A good practice regarding evaluation is to do that yearly. It is important to determine if you are growing with the expectations and demands of ministry that have come about. Identify where you might be lagging, and develop a plan to grow your skill in that area. Every year it is important to ask:

- What changes in my activities do I find rewarding and satisfying?
- How have my public presentations matured?
- Do I learn as I prepare to teach? Why or why not?
- What am I calling persons toward in my discipling ministry?
- To what extent are my relationships with leaders stronger or weaker?
- How faithful am I in the aspects of ministry that are not easy for me?

All of these questions can sometimes help us not only to determine that staying is the correct answer but also to understand how staying can give us renewed purpose and satisfaction in ministry.

Evaluations are best done in context; that is, not one of us is good at everything. Our skills and abilities need to be assessed in the light the circumstances in which we find ourselves. In other words, a sermon that might be deemed excellent at a church in a college town might be considered a terrible sermon in a rural parish church. Likewise, never calling on parishioners in their homes might be considered fine in an urban setting but is considered totally missing the work of the pastor in a small town. We could go on and on with examples along this line.

Evaluating ministry is most helpful when the system we serve, as well as the work of the individual pastor, is being assessed. It is important to measure your effectiveness and the engagement and response of those to whom you minister. Evaluations will be more meaningful when there is not major conflict present and (did we mention?) when it is done regularly.

We recommend that evaluation begin after the first six months of the ministry. This is to assess whether there is a match between the perceived needs of the congregation as articulated to the pastor and the perceived skills of the pastor. Or, in the case of another ministry position, evaluation determines whether the needs of the position and the work of the minister are being fulfilled. Often people will say everything is going well and may not want to do an evaluation in fear that the evaluation itself may upset the apple cart. However, if everything is going well, evaluation at that end of the first six months provides an opportunity to acknowledge success and to be sure everything is in place for a long relationship.

Regular evaluation can help you assess whether or not there need to be adjustments in performance or priorities. It may help a pastor to decide what continuing education events she ought to be looking for to hone her skills for the benefit of the congregation. Best evaluations are based on the criteria and goals that have been determined. We strongly urge that the church have a job description for the pastor and other ministry positions. Evaluations should be based on the job description. If the job description indicates that the pastor should be involved in denominational life, then it is fair to ask a question about that on the evaluation. In assessing the evaluation, the team doing the work may well find areas that need to be addressed in the job description or in the work of the church. Regular evaluation will give you the choice of staying or going in response to God's call. Not doing evaluation may all too often cause you to leave for reasons other than a divine summons.

Ministers are also encouraged to do a spiritual evaluation each year. How is your spiritual life doing? What skills do you need to add to be spiritually healthy? What discipline do you need to practice that will keep you spiritually healthy? This spiritual check-up is important to identify if the inner stirring you are sensing is to transition in ministry or to mature and feed your walk with Christ. A healthy practice of evaluation and accountability is the first step in making good ministry decisions on a daily basis and certainly can help us as we face a more major decision as to whether or not we are in the best ministry place for us at any given time.

## Bivocational Church Ministry

At the crossroads of ministry transition, several options may be considered. One is moving to another full-time, church-based ministry setting. Another viable option is bivocational ministry. Church-based ministry in a part-time role is both demanding and rewarding. It is demanding of time and energy, because it is in addition to your other employment. It is easily defendable to say that full-time church-based ministry doesn't pay very well, and as easily defendable to say that part-time ministry pays very well. Bivocational ministry plays an increasingly significant role in the life of churches, because many small and medium-size churches are experiencing significant financial pressure. Quite often these churches can afford to pay a responsible salary but can't afford the health insurance and retirement benefits required by most full-time candidates. Bivocational ministry allows the church to live within its means and have quality ministry. In *The Work of the Bivocational Minister,* Dennis Bickers gives a thorough and insightful explanation of bivocational ministry. He makes the valid claim that all ministries, whether full-time or part-time, have value and provide ministry to those in need.

In our experience, the position most in demand is a trained person for bivocational ministry. Increasingly churches are squeezed financially and can't pay a full salary and benefit package. Additionally, many congregations are not large enough to keep a minister busy if they could afford a fully funded minister. Bivocational ministry is demanding because you will have competing loyalties. But it provides vital ministry, often with minimal travel. It often is an intentional choice for quality of life. Choosing bivocational ministry means providing availability of your service to the church, often a service much appreciated.

One way to do bivocational ministry is to do it as a ministry specialist. Some specialists include interim ministers, church planters, hospice chaplains, and parish nurses.

## Making a Career Change

Although it is sometimes the assumption that we are talking about pastors moving from one congregation to another, another option is a change in profession. If full-time, church-based ministry is not fulfilling and satisfying to you and your family, then a change in professions may be your choice. Riley has often described ministry as "rubbing on God's grace and mercy," meaning that the context of ministry is not particularly important to the God who called you. How we do the work we are called to do is more important to God than the setting in which we are doing the work. One may minister as pastor of a church while another ministers as teacher in a junior high school—and the latter may touch more lives (and need more of God's wisdom and grace) than the former!

Where clergy go when they make a career change is quite varied. Choosing a second career needs to be as intentional as choosing the first. There are many professions where care and serving can be expressed: health care, teaching, social work, advocacy and justice work, or other not-for-profit positions are examples.

If you have decided to make a career change, begin by examining your interests and your skills. A primary resource bank to consider is your transferable skills.[1] Some transferable skills are those such as teaching, encouraging, selling, and listening. Other transferable skills may be ones that you have developed through various jobs, volunteer work, hobbies, and experiences. Each of us has a secular work history, if we will take time to identify it, including those summer jobs, jobs during school, or the time between degrees. We each have a strange collection of experiences: working in an icehouse, life guarding, on-air radio experience, selling x-ray equipment. When you look at your experiences, focus on the skill (for instance, public speaking, persuading rather than preaching) rather than the context. This will free up your thinking. You can bring skills such as conflict management, administration, budgeting, public speaking, counseling and care, specialized ministry areas (children, youth, seniors, couples), or leadership to any secular context.

Do a skills assessment, and then research occupations that can utilize those skills and interests. Learn as much as you can about the occupations that match your skills. Talk to people in that business to test the match of your skills. Read job and career profiles. Be sure to consider how your personal values will fit in a particular career.

Identify what additional training you will need to enter and succeed in this career. Begin to develop a network of persons who are both leaders and practitioners in this business. Carefully choose a mentor to help you prepare educationally and emotionally. Begin the educational preparation while you are in your ministry. It may or may not be necessary to complete the training before you can get a job in your chosen field. Develop a clear plan that maps out your strategy. Take into consideration relocation, finances, and the time needed to accomplish a job search.[2]

Develop a new résumé that identifies both objectives and skills. This résumé will be different from your previous ones; make sure to research the résumé expectations of the career you are seeking. Research the industry and the individual companies or organizations you interview with. It is important to ask questions about contemporary issues specific to the company that is considering you. Your search can take several months. Be patient, and do not become discouraged. God is with you in this change as surely as all the other changes in your life. Valerie K. Isenhower and Judith A. Todd have co-authored a wonderful book on spiritual discernment: *Living into the Answers: A Workbook for Personal Spiritual Discernment.*

This transition to the secular workplace may feel foreign to you. But in all likelihood you have been there before. Most of us held various jobs during our formal education. It will also be useful to remember what you may have taught and encouraged about ministry in the workplace. Remember that God calls all God's children to serve; just because you may be serving outside the church does not diminish the service. And, there may be advantages that aren't available in the local church, such as a regular workday or one supervisor instead of a board. Be prepared to begin at entry level. Your well-developed skill bank and hard work should allow you to advance.

Whatever choices you face, remember that we are suggesting you do nothing without prayer and sacred discernment. Any call decision is a spiritual decision. All the elements before you are part of that spiritual decision. The items that you have discerned that must be or must not be are part of this spiritual discernment process.

Many persons find fulfillment of their call to ministry serving in a Christian organization. Christian higher education provides opportunities for professional educators and administrators. Christian camping has enormous appeal to many persons. Another context that is emerging is ministry in the workplace. Police, fire, and industrial chaplaincy are examples. Military chaplaincy has been around the longest and has many advantages. In *The Work of the Chaplain,* Naomi Paget and Janet McCormack offer essential understanding of this critical caregiver role in a variety of public contexts.

## Networking

Networking is an important component of pastoral moves. This includes even the move to other forms of ministry, such as chaplaincy or denominational or nonprofit agencies. One should always be aware that building one's network is important. Fortunately or unfortunately, it is important sometimes who we know. Again, it is assumed that we all build our relationships because it is in our nature to build good relationships, but sometimes those relationships can help us get our feet in the door at some churches or agencies. It is wise to keep this in mind throughout our lives, rather than because we suddenly have a desire to make a move. We also need to keep this in mind for other people. We can be important relationships for them, we too are a part of a network, and it can and does work both ways.

Sometimes the hardest part of responding to God's call to a ministry different from the local church is the myth that only pastoral ministry is real ministry. It is difficult to be in the teaching position of telling people that bivocational or other ministry is just as legitimate as pastoral ministry: you are still called to be a teacher or social worker or whatever. If you know this call is from God, we encourage you in voicing this call to others. God calls many to many different places. Interpret your call, and do not be discouraged.

## Applying the Principles

### Adjustment

Eli was a long-time bivocational minister. His first experience out of seminary was extremely painful for his spouse. Subsequently he went to work in the family-owned auto dealership. This provided for his family's needs and the needs of his extended family. The context of their business allowed him to serve nearby churches over a period of thirty years. He never had to travel more than thirty miles from home. His seminary training and business experience made him a very capable minister.

### Looking Ahead

Gayle's church was active in community ministries, and something was always going on. Three years into her first ministry, the church remodeled the sanctuary. Gayle realized that she felt unprepared to lead the church in its task-oriented ministry. She also realized that this issue would be even more significant if she were to move to a larger congregation. She began to focus her reading on leadership and creating a common vision. The local vocational school offered a couple of courses in project management. While the focus of the course work was business-oriented, she felt she would pick up skills and insights that would be transferable to a ministry context.

## Suggestions for Your *Next Steps*

- What possibilities are you considering at this time? God calls us to places where we fit and are delighted in our work.
- What gives you delight?
- What would you love to be doing professionally?

## Suggestions for *Prayer*

- Thank God for your present ministry and for those with whom and to whom you minister.
- Ask God to lead you as you go forward in ministry.

• Ask God to put opportunities in your path and people who will help you as you consider your call.

• Ask God to lay upon your heart the people God would have you serve.

NOTES

1. Dawn Rosenberg McKay, "Guide to Career Planning," About.com, http://careerplanning.about.com/od/careerchoicechan/a/transferable.htm (accessed November 12, 2010).

2. "Ten Tips on Making a Successful Career Change," http://www .allbusiness.com/human-resources/careers-changing-jobs/1618-1.html (accessed November 12, 2010).

# CHAPTER 4
# Forced Out

The disagreement became so sharp that they parted company; Barnabas took Mark with him and sailed away to Cyprus. But Paul chose Silas and set out, the believers commending him to the grace of the Lord. (Acts 15:39-40)

*Up to this point,* we have chosen to be even-handed in our discussion of the various issues of transitions in ministry. But when you've been forced out of a church, everything, it seems, is different. The transition becomes far more painful for the minister, the minister's family, and for others involved in the transition—going and coming.

There are all kinds of reasons a pastor might be forced out of a ministry. Economics may have changed, and the church cannot afford the previous level of support. The decision may have been reached honestly by the church. In many cases, the church may have used economics as an excuse. Real or imagined slights, real or imagined work concerns, and real or imagined events can all lead to the pastor being dismissed. An individual, a family, or a group may unilaterally and for his or her personal interest assert control in the church. Firing a minister may be done by as few as one person.

A church may have to dismiss a minister who is selfishly and recklessly damaging a church. In this situation, the church has the obligation and need to protect itself. Riley knew one pastor who always left clergy meetings with the same comment: "I am off to persecute the saints." It turned out that he wasn't joking. He was abusing the congregation.

Forced exits occur in a mixture of forms. Just over 10 percent of forced exits are terminations. Slightly less than two-thirds are forced resignations, and in about one-third of the cases there is direct pressure to resign. Forced exits occur across the span of a ministry career. Fully one-third of clergy experience a forced exit in their first ministry. More than half of clergy experience forced terminations in their second or third ministry context. And about one-fourth of clergy experience a forced exit in their fourth, fifth, or sixth ministry.[1]

A whole book could be developed on this issue alone, but within the scope of this volume, we cannot attempt to deal with such a traumatic event in a comprehensive way. Primarily, we want to offer hope and hints to the minister who is forced to seek the next calling. This hope is offered in two forms. The first is to say that not all churches are the same. It may be that the problems in one church will not be so in the next. The second is that God is in the equation, and there will be a tomorrow that has promise for you. Keep your focus on God's call on your life. Make sure the careers you consider are in harmony with your values and will provide satisfaction. Revisit earlier career options that you considered to see if they are good choices for you now.

Whatever the specific circumstances or timing, being forced out or fired from a ministry position is a shattering experience. It threatens the security we have of financially supporting our family. It threatens our ability to trust the church and the people of the church. It threatens our sense of call and our trust in the God who called us. As a crisis of faith, it will necessarily cause re-examination of many of our personal or family foundational beliefs and goals.

In these situations a minister doesn't just lose a job. The pastor and family lose their church, their friends, and often their house. They lose their place in their identified community. The many aspects of loss compound the trauma experienced by the minister and the family.

As ministers, we have chosen a relationship with the church and congregation of profound trust and dependence. Being rejected and cast out of that relationship can often cause a sense of spiritual violation. The church that we trusted to accept and love us has cast us aside. It may even seem that the God we trust, in the form of the employing church, betrayed our response to what we felt was a call from God.[2]

Because of shame or pain, the church wants to close the chapter and try to quickly move away from these events. There is an unfortunate tendency to sanitize personal and corporate memory. Furthermore, church leaders may mistakenly believe that holding the "angries" to account will cause more damage. This failure to confront has the same effect as condoning the action does.

The minister might be threatened or told to keep quiet or risk losing potential severance. Often there is a one-sided appeal to the minister not to do anything to "split the church." The minister is urged to respond according to an urgent schedule that is presented as being best for everyone. Expedience causes the pressuring entity to want to ignore work agreements or church governance documents. There is a tendency to want to agree on a scripted misrepresentation of the real reasons for the actions.

If an end to a current ministry is imminent, conduct yourself as much as possible in a manner consistent with your calling to ministry. All of the parties will benefit if the separation can be conducted in a way that is decent and orderly. Inviting a third party to facilitate communication and agreements will assist everyone involved. Because communication is already stressed, be sure that all agreements are in writing.

## An Exit Agreement

An exit agreement should address the following points:

- Ending date of ministry
- Date by which receipts or mileage records must be submitted for reimbursement
- The dismissed employee must agree to not talk negatively or behave badly toward the church or other staff persons. Violation of this element will negate the rest of the agreement.

- The church and leaders must agree not to talk negatively or behave badly toward the exiting minister.

- The severance package:
  —how much will be paid
  —when and how the payments will be made

- Date by which health insurance coverage ends

- If the minister lives in church-provided housing:
  —when the property will be vacated
  —who will pay utilities
  —who will receive the keys when the minister leaves
  —the date by which personal property will be removed from church property

- When payments to minister's retirement will cease

The need for a written exit agreement as presented in this section focuses on forced exits from ministry and is very important in this context. It is also wise to use such a written agreement in any transition from a ministry. It can help avoid problems caused by acting on assumptions by either party. (Find a sample agreement online at www.judsonpress.com/free_download.) Communication is hindered by the stress of grief and change in all ministry transitions.

## The Forced-Out Family

Your spouse and children will suffer differently; they often are more removed from firsthand information and options of how to respond than is the minister. The minister may have peers or denominational resources, but the spouse and children have been cut off from the vast majority of their social and spiritual friends. Often, as the primary focus of the church's rejection, you as the minister are too deeply hurt to respond in a helpful manner to your family. The minister, spouse, and family will likely experience depression. You need to be prepared to get you and your family into supportive counseling after being forced out of a church-based ministry.

Just as a physician is not the best medical caregiver for her family, so a pastor is not the best spiritual caregiver for her family. One reason to move the family as soon as possible into another faith community is to find someone to help them process their wounds and concerns. More clergy children have been lost to the faith because of actions of churches than can be numbered.

As soon as you can, be as transparent as you can with your spouse and your children. Accept your own responsibility. Affirm the goodness of God and the frailty of God's people. As bad as your situation is, remember that God's specialty is redemption.

## Collateral Damage

Most often neither the congregation nor the "angries" who act on their own count the whole costs of dismissing the pastor. The church itself can often sustain collateral damage. In a disagreeable church situation, the first recourse is to avoid getting to a stage that is beyond hope. But always through the struggle the pastor should remember that there is more at stake than this particular ministry; there is the faith and faith life of people in the congregation who may have nothing to do with the struggle. Protecting those people as best as possible is part of ministry in these painful struggles. Helping people keep their faith intact is an important ministry in the face of sometimes overwhelming pain. Remember that the call to pastoral care of the vulnerable and bewildered members is still important, and it is important to give care rather than bring these people into the fray. There is so much at stake in a church fight, and a good pastor will remember that his or her first duty is to do the work of God within the faith community.

Persons in church life who are early in their spiritual journey will often be disillusioned and may quit participating in church after a church fight. The emerging leaders learn "dismissal of clergy" is an easy escape from facing the challenges of being church in their setting. Emerging leaders are part of the collateral damage; they are drawn into participating in the falsehood that this is "best for the church." Persons they trust and look up to use them for their own purpose.

Young people and children can turn away from a call to ministry because of how ministers in their lives have been treated. The witness of the church in the community is damaged. Virtually every dismissal divides a congregation. Individual wounds heal slowly; corporate wounds heal more slowly.

Remember during such a time to keep your focus on God. Put more time into your prayer life. Ask your family, friends, and colleagues to be in prayer with you. Be sure to keep appropriate boundaries around the issue, but bring the resources God has given you in the situation to bear. If you are part of a denomination, be in touch as early as possible with the judicatory for assistance with the problem. The resources they can share at times like these can make a difference throughout the process. They may help in bringing grace to an otherwise graceless situation. If you are not part of a denomination, ask for help from your colleagues in the community. Ask for advice; share your concerns and fears. If the time comes to negotiate with the church, ask someone to accompany you and help you see realities and possibilities. Use these same resources as you seek to build new résumés and find new opportunities for service.

As you leave this stressed situation, we invite you to remember the community in which the church is situated. Remember to say good-bye and thank you to the community people who have contributed to your ministry. It may be difficult, but this simple task may serve you well in the future.

This is a time that you might practice the Eastern saying, "A problem is really an opportunity." You must do the homework to discover the truth for you. If you have been forced out of a church, we highly recommend that you explore information about yourself and your performance before you seek another call.

## Fearless Assessment

As soon as possible, we as clergy must begin a fearless inventory of what we contributed to the situation. The score is never 100 to 0; it is never all their fault or our entire fault. We must identify and accept our portion of the responsibility that led to termination. Our portion may have been sins of commission or omission. Our pride may have prevented us from addressing the stated needs or desired ministries. A termination will almost always have deep roots. It can be said that you have already paid for this learning opportunity; redeem this painful experience by learning as much as possible.

We need to address what has happened with several steps. The first step is to become clear about what has happened before you take another ministry. If another ministry presents itself, be honest with yourself. You have some hurts to work through, so develop a plan to work through them—for instance, see a counselor, spiritual director, or coach.

We highly recommend that you attend a center for ministry or other such career-counseling place. The staff there can help you to assess your skills and gifts and determine if the ministry position you held was right for you. They can also help you to assess what you might need to look for in your next ministry setting. The center can give help to your spouse as well. Above all, get help in two areas: grief counseling and career counseling,

Another resource is colleagues who are ready to stand next to someone hurting and in pain. They can be your first line of assistance. They can be with you in everyday ministry, and they can stand with you in times of trouble. We know of pastors who in times of pain reached out to colleagues and there found a variety of assistance, from good listening ears to invitations to their church for an evangelistic week (thus putting a few dollars in the pocket of the person who has been dismissed). Spouses and families of colleagues can also be ministers to your spouse and family. Remember this resource in ministry when you have need.

If we are too damaged by the event to make it a real-time learning opportunity, we need to get away for a time to clear our heads and heal our wounds. Go into another line of work for a time. You may find that this might work better for you. You might find that there are some part-time positions that suit you and that doing something else during the other time gives you perspective and hope for the pastorate or other ministry task.

Also remember that there is a variety of ministry calls. Our call can be interpreted in many ways, and sometimes we need to reinterpret it in a way that finds that the job we can get can become our ministry. Reframing can help us all. Our call to ministry is more defining than our understanding of our call to a specific form of ministry. Honor the call, but be responsive to the many possible shapes of response.

Another possibility is returning to or going to school. Upgrading your credentials, attending a residential Clinical Pastoral Education (CPE) course, or getting a master's or postgraduate degree in a particular program might be the answer to your frustration about ministry. There are many possibilities, and there are scholarships and ways to finance this if it is the next step for you.

Above all, do not let the pain of losing a ministry position affect your faith and belief in God. Keep hold of the faith. Remember that God loves you and wants the best for you. We human beings do not always keep our eyes on God, and the church is full of human beings. Just because we are in the church does not mean that the church will always do things right or fairly. Be gentle with yourself and with those you might perceive has having hurt you; they, too, are God's children.

Being forced out is traumatic if your employing organization forces the conclusion upon you that you are in the wrong place. But if you are feeling that things are wrong, take steps yourself. If you make the decision, you will have more time and energy to make a considered life transition. You and your family can have more control of your life and circumstances. It might be easy to feel trapped in ministry because that is the sum of our experience and the focus of our education. In reality, ministry may have honed skills that can be used in other contexts. People skills, planning skills, responding to emergencies, functioning without tight supervision, interpersonal and public communication skills, and intervention skills can be repackaged for your next career path.

Entering into a discovery process informed by outplacement professionals can be most useful. This process will assist with skills assessment, job compatibility for persons with your interests, and development of a strategy for an orderly and successful transition. Outplacement services are helpful because you will receive assistance in refocusing career options and guidance in the necessary steps to gain employment. If you are related to a denomination, they might have specific places where you can get away to do the thinking and reflecting that are needed after a painful departure. There are also nondenominational sites and resources set up for pastors. You might even identify and complete training or a degree program that would prepare you for the transition while serving a church.

Facing the crossroads in ministry is sometimes a difficult task. It is made more difficult if we are forced out, but it can be difficult even if we are offered a wonderful opportunity. We must still face the letting go of one ministry and the taking on of ministry in our next place. No matter what the place in ministry—another church, another ministry (chaplain, hospice care), or a secular setting—we need to keep focused on our relationship with God. Making a move with the assurance that God blesses and goes with us in the move provides hope and possibilities even when we hit rough places in the next ministry setting.

## Applying the Principles

### Outplacement

Larry had three two-year ministries. He worked hard and prayerfully going about his ministry, but he never could avoid conflict with his lay leaders. He tried every way he knew; he listened and did what they asked him to do. When that didn't work, he presented ideas that were rejected. In frustration he began a new ministry focus and didn't take a proposal to his board. Nothing he did worked. He wasn't getting even cost-of-living raises. Reflecting on his short, frustrating, and often painful ministries, he went to his judicatory staff person to talk about what was and wasn't working. They talked and prayed and eventually concluded that it would be best for Larry and his family to look for a nonpastoral job that allowed him to be involved in caregiving. With financial support from his judicatory, he went to a specialist in outplacement. That process and previous volunteer experiences led him to apply for and be hired as director of a county care and disaster assistance agency. In this context he had general oversight by his board, but no one micromanaged his work. His family benefited from not living in a local church fishbowl. He also found significant opportunities for ministry as a volunteer in his local church. While the salaries and benefits were the same in Larry's new work, he did have to make adjustments in his finances; he realized he would not have the deduction of a full housing allowance.

### Starting Over

Richard, a committed but average student, was eager to finish seminary and enter ministry. He was called to his first church, a call to which he responded with great excitement and energy. It is hard to say why, but his ministry started off badly and then got worse. Everything he tried to do didn't satisfy folks. The harder he tried, the worse it got. After eleven months, the church terminated him. Richard left confused and hurt by the rejection.

Richard went back to his hometown and the church he grew up in. He considered Pastor Bill to be his mentor. He went to Pastor Bill and said, "I messed up, but I am not sure what I was doing wrong. Will you help me figure out what went wrong and how I can fix it?" They worked together for about two years. Richard did a lot of growing up as he accepted responsibility for what he had done wrong and what he could do that would allow him to have a meaningful ministry. He sought another church. This time he was able to hear his leaders and respond to their input. He learned to be faithful in visitation and empowering others to minister. Richard never did become the best minister in town, but he had learned from his bad experience and didn't make the same fatal mistakes he had made in his first ministry.

## Suggestions for Your *Next Steps*

- Have you asked for help from denominational or ministry colleagues? Why or why not?
- What have you done to bring God into the equation?
- If things are already at loggerheads in your congregation, what are you (and other church leaders) doing to get help?

- How effectively are you able to continue to minister appropriately to those not in the conflict? How are you reassuring family, young people, new leaders, and others that God is still with your congregation and that faith and hope are still present and at work?

- How are you taking care of yourself and your family in the midst of the situation? What could you do additionally or differently to improve that self-care?

- What do you need to do to make things better right now?

## Suggestions for *Prayer*

- Thank God for the ministry you have.

- Thank God for all the people in the church, including those who are giving you grief. Pray especially for those giving you grief that God will make God's self known to them and bring them hope and peace.

- Thank God for leading you in the past and ask God to continue to lead you through this valley of terror; remember to affirm God's presence though all trouble. Where you cannot pray with honesty, ask God to help your unbelief.

- Pray for your family; pray for those who are vulnerable to loss of faith in these troubled times.

- Express thanksgiving for God's promise to always be present.

NOTES

1. "Forced Exits: High-Risk Churches," http://www.christianitytoday.com/yc/more/specialreport/6y3072.html (accessed September 9, 2010).

2. Nancy Myers Hopkins, *The Congregation Is Also a Victim* (Bethesda, MD: The Alban Institute, 1993), 11.

# CHAPTER 5
# Church-Specific Matters

As he walked by the Sea of Galilee, he saw two brothers, Simon, who is called Peter, and Andrew his brother, casting a net into the sea—for they were fishermen. And he said to them, "Follow me, and I will make you fish for people." Immediately they left their nets and followed him. (Matthew 4:18-20)

*We live in a harried culture.* We expect immediate delivery on items we purchase. We schedule our children in back-to-back activities every school-day afternoon. In too many cases we let church life mimic the frantic pace of the culture. Discerning God's calling is countercultural. We can't make this decision while driving between family activities. Discerning God's call takes longer than a phone call. In considering an invitation to another ministry, we must seek to understand the church or organization, its members, and their uniqueness. We must consider our self and our family living and working in that specific context. We must gather information, prayerfully consider, and immerse ourselves in the best understanding we can get. We must look to see if God would have us there to serve and lead.

We have already established that as a minister in transition, you need to know yourself in order to discern the kind of ministry setting best suited to your gifts, your experience, and your call. With that foundational knowledge secure, it is time to consider how you will assess the ministry placement(s) that may become available. Throughout this book, we have tried to paint in broad strokes the ministry settings available to you as a minister of Jesus Christ, but in this chapter, we focus more specifically on unique aspects of the parish setting. We will endeavor to highlight those issues that have application in other ministry contexts, but when we do focus on congregational life, we trust that ministers considering other contexts will extrapolate from the principles we discuss.

## Organizational Employment History

An organization's history can tell you a lot about the kind of leader it values, as well as the kind of treatment a leader may expect. When considering a call to a specific ministry, you will want to learn the answers to questions such as these:

- What leadership style did the previous pastor have?
- How long was the tenure of the previous pastor?
- Who is serving as pastor now—an interim, an assistant, a retiring pastor, or a lay leader?
- What is the average tenure of previous pastors?
- How long were the longest and shortest pastorates in the last thirty years?

Some congregations are clergy healers, and some rather consistently do damage to their clergy. The ethos of some congregations empowers and encourages their ministers to grow and mature. Other congregations consistently offer judgment and pain. Congregations can attempt to transfer all of their anxieties and failures on the clergy who serve them. Their history is littered with the debris of discarded and damaged clergy. It is important to know the conditions under which former ministers left. We need to ask the search committee, denominational sources, and nearby clergy if some ministers were fired. Were others forced out? This is important, because we are not immune to either arrogance or ignorance. We often say, "That won't happen to me" or "I can handle it." But knowing what you are getting into will allow you to be prepared for some things when they come along. You will be much more likely to do well if you know the history of a congregation than to assume that you can do well in all situations.

John C. Larue Jr. asserts that one in four churches has terminated five or more ministers in its history. A majority of churches (62 percent) that have terminated a pastor are repeat offenders.[1] The presenting issues in a termination often don't justify this repeated solution of convenience. The whole congregation often isn't told the whole truth, and a group of as few as five persons can force a pastor out. The congregations as well as the clergy are damaged. Ask both the search committee and denominational sources: How many former ministers have been terminated or forced out, and why? If the answer is more than one or two in the last fifteen years, take caution.

We are not saying that you should not serve such a church, but you should research why this occurs and prepare for it if you choose to serve the church. Preparation means setting up an accountability group that understands your concerns and can help you when problems strike. This accountability group most likely would not include anyone in the church; instead, it should be made up of nearby clergy colleagues, maybe your regional minister, trusted friends, and perhaps your spouse. This group should meet at least once a quarter, if not monthly. Make the meetings a priority, and ask that the other members make it priority. Be honest with this group about what you see happening in the church. When a situation develops that has potential to get ugly, call the group together for an emergency meeting so you can address the issues as soon as possible with the wise counsel and prayers of this accountability group. You may never need to call an emergency meeting, but it will be helpful to have this group's support and encouragement as you work with such a congregation.

Following either a long or a short tenure of a predecessor will bring unique issues. It is important to gain the church's understanding of the reasons for a short tenure. Were the ministry and the exit abrasive? Were there ethical or moral breaches on the part of the minister? This will cause the congregation to withhold trust from the successor. If the minister just left and the church isn't clear about the causes, trust of the successor's call to ministry and commitment to ministry may be withheld.

When you follow a long pastorate, the pitfalls are more diffuse and hard to define. A congregation can be conflicted in its feelings about the previous pastor. Part of their heart accepts that the pastor left or retired. Another part of their heart doesn't want to make room for a new pastor. Persons often complain about change and the pace of change, even if only the voice has changed. The persons who follow a long tenure might endure rejection at various levels of intensity. You must have a tenacious commitment to wait until the system is willing to accept you as pastor. Acceptance may be incremental, so you must value the little steps of progress.

## Culture and Community

The social culture in which the church is located and where the people are conditioned shape the nature of church life. Constituents bring their worldview and values to the life of the congregation. The culture of a gown town (college community) is different from a community near a major military installation, which is different from a rural county seat. Naturally, churches located in each of those communities will also have distinctive cultures. An organizational culture that is common to members by employment, affinity, or common rejection of certain norms can define church life. Smaller rural churches tend to be more homogeneous, with members who share professional or organizational ties in an economy dominated by farming or factory or small business. Urban congregations may be equally small but far more diverse in socioeconomic class, professional and educational backgrounds, and even ethnic identity. As a minister considering a move to a specific opportunity, you must access your ability to live and work in its sociocultural context.

One of the most challenging local ministry sites Marcia knows is in the Fremont neighborhood of Seattle. Urban neighborhoods are difficult in and of themselves. In the Fremont neighborhood, there is a plaque in the neighborhood that declares that it is the center of the universe. The neighborhood hosts an annual solstice day festival in June, complete with an unofficial naked bike ride. Fremont Baptist Church, the only and oldest church structure in the neighborhood, is one block from the Aurora Bridge Troll.

Doing ministry in this quirky culture takes someone who is aware of what she can or cannot do.

One of the worst disconnects between church and pastor in Marcia's experience happened because a pastor and the church did not take into consideration cultural differences when they made a call. A West Coast church in a town dominated by a military facility was out of the cultural understanding of a pastor who had spent his entire life in West Virginia. He was astounded at the cost of sending his children to a Christian school, and the church members were astounded that he was not happy to send his children to their public schools. Then there was his lack of understanding of the city in general. He did not understand the military mindset of the community, let alone the western independence of the people in the community. The pastor did not stay long and returned to West Virginia.

In general, community size and proximity to a larger community will influence church life. In a farming community, it is hard to have midweek congregational meals and activities. Congregants with fixed work schedules can more easily accommodate midweek activities. In urban congregations, you may have neighborhood churches where you might schedule things through the week. But there are those larger urban congregations where activities need to happen in clusters so that people have to travel in only once or twice. Both culture and personal schedules shape the members' expectation of church life. The lifestyle and values of the people of the church often indicate what kind of lifestyle and values they will expect their pastor to have. You will never be entirely free from lifestyle expectations of the congregation. Do your best to find a fit to your lifestyle and values for a ministry that will bring satisfaction and give understanding and hope.

## Needs of the Pastoral Family

Pastoral families' needs and values play an important part in choosing what kind of church community you will consider. A small community located far from a larger community may not meet clergy family needs. If there are health issues in the clergy family that require specialized care, don't create an ongoing crisis by locating far away from adequate health facilities. The needs of academically gifted children or the need by either spouse to complete education should be considered in choosing a place to relocate.

Perhaps you and your spouse choose to be a single-income family, preferring that your spouse be primary caregiver to young children or aging parents. This decision offers rich benefits to your family, but it will also have an opportunity cost. Some congregations are unable to fund fully a full-time pastor, and very few can afford to pay a salary sufficient to support a family.

An emerging reality needing consideration is two-career couples. Considering employment opportunities for your spouse is part of honoring God's work in the life of each person in the relationship. Both persons securing fulfilling employment will affect personal satisfaction and meeting economic needs and goals. Some careers are portable; some are not.

In the case of clergy couples, geography can be very important. Are there opportunities for both clergy? Are you as a couple willing to serve in different denominations? Do both employing congregations understand and accept that the spouse will likely be in another congregation? Ministry transitions for clergy couples often require one clergy to receive a call at one time and then wait for the other to receive a call.

Another issue that must be considered is what Marcia calls the need for a "culture fix." Does a given community or proximity to a cultural center meet your family's expectations regarding opportunities to experience symphony, concerts, museums, theater, art galleries, or other cultural events? How you and your family respond to the community to which you move makes a difference. Sometimes moves across country work well. Other times people find that the cultural differences between the East Coast, the West Coast, and the Midwest are unexpected and uncomfortable. Marcia lives in western Washington, which has a reputation of always having rain; if you have a need for sun, this is not the climate you would want. If you appreciate a culture where the church and clergy are consulted and listened to, it is not in western Washington. The climate and the culture of the community can make a difference to how you and your family may feel about the new ministry.

## Leadership Styles

There are many instruments and written materials that can help us define and determine our preferred leadership style. We must know that the style we use is authentic for us and is not mimicking a respected person or pattern. We've already indicated that ministry style and congregational size are closely linked. What are the expectations of the system you serve? It is essential that we understand that leadership is always in context. The leadership requirements for a small gown-town church filled with PhDs are going to be different from those for a small church in a mixed-income suburb of a large city. We need to have the understanding and flexibility to exert leadership in a context-sensitive manner.

Leadership skills are easily transferable to nonparish contexts. Riley had conversations with a college instructor who was leaving that position but didn't have a focus of where she might go. During the conversation she said she taught leadership. Riley commented, "Leadership is leadership; you have other options outside of teaching." Subsequently he found out she had taken a job as superintendent of schools in another state.

Understanding what engages the leadership part of our personality is important. For Riley it is responsibility. If he is the one responsible or perceives himself responsible, he engages as a leader. If he doesn't perceive himself as responsible, he can go with the flow as participant. His wife is a nurse who worked many years in coronary care. With her around, he never worried what he would do if someone had a coronary problem. He just made room for her to work and did what she told him to do.

It is necessary to know where in the organizational system we need to be leader and where we need to be participant. Does the leadership style you exhibit have flexibilities? It is reasonable to expect that one would exert different leadership styles in different situations. Even in situations where you are not the appointed leader, your leadership may differ. For instance, at a bridal shower you might offer a blessing for the bride or offer grace before refreshments, whereas at a building fire you might assist in crowd control, offer pastoral presence with family members or responders, and follow through with victims. Can you select the style for the situation, or do you rigidly manifest a preferred style?

Churches may find ways to get around a leadership style that is not a complement with its style. One church chose to have committee meetings without notifying the pastor, because the pastor exercised only a controlling leadership style. It is helpful if you can develop a flexible style according to the needs and gifts of the congregation. We are edifying lay leaders when we give them the chance to succeed, fail, and learn on their own. If folks are engaging and growing, coaching will empower those efforts. Remember, a significant goal in ministry is to train ourselves out of a job. We need to be careful not to confuse leadership with a personal need to control. We need to refer again to the leadership needs of the size of church we are serving or considering serving; do we have those skills and abilities in our skill set? Can we find ways to add them to our skill set?

## Team Ministry

Considering a ministry that calls for multiple staff demands reflection and flexibility from persons considering the position as lead pastor or ministry specialist. The demands are different, but each must consider what is expected. And with every team the expectations can be different. Marcia Bailey has written a book about ministry partnership that describes one kind of team ministry that takes the word "partnership" seriously. But the next ministry situation may develop a different kind of team or partnership ministry.[2] Persons considering positions that demand sharing the scope of ministry must be prepared and able to work in cooperation. Clergy who can't or won't delegate responsibility and authority will struggle in any kind of team ministry. Supervising pastors must be able to focus on what, not how. Micromanaging staff is inefficient and unfulfilling for persons who serve with you. Control gives a direct message: "You aren't trusted."

To be effective and empowering to other persons we must be able to let ministry happen beyond the reach of our hands and our sight; this is as true for staff as it is for lay leaders. In order to be fulfilled serving on a staff, one must be willing not to have total control. Team ministry has many manifestations. Sometimes it means doing what you are told; in other contexts it may mean team collaboration and consensus. The reality that one encounters is a combination of the expectations of the senior pastor and the congregation, and whether one is staff or the senior pastor it is important to determine the style that is expected in a given situation.

One needs to have conversations with current and past staff members in order to understand the operative rules. You need to know how other professionals have experienced the situation you are considering. No two people experience a situation in the same way, but you can glean the essence of that setting. Team ministry can break down because of the supervisor's limits, staff person's limits, or staff culture. Usually it is a combination of all three. The ability to trust and communicate is essential in being successful as a team. It has been both Marcia's and Riley's experience that working in a team context has been a blessing and a curse, but it is always necessary to accomplish the ministry needs of the congregational or organizational systems.

## Worship

Worship is often the one place in church life where all generations gather. Even in congregations that provide multiple styles of worship, the norm, values, and congregational ethos shape worship. Inexperienced clergy often attempt to change the worship experience to fit their comfort zone and preferences. The competition among worship styles is far more than song selection and "Do we or do we not use hymnals?" It is a matter of learning and communication styles of different generations. When going on a journey, we have to start where we are. Worship is a community experience and should be shaped by community input.

The most complete meltdown in a congregation Riley has seen arose from the pastor's strengths that were overplayed. The pastor, who was quite gifted in liturgical worship, was a strong introvert and was spiritually fed by contemplative worship that was in contrast to the tradition and preference of a majority of the congregation. The pastor was absolutely unbending in the worship he planned and led. He was closed to input from congregational leaders and congregants. This led to divisions along previously existing fault lines in the congregation. The congregation became paralyzed, and the pastor left. This left behind a family of faith that had to reconstruct itself, its relationships, and its ministry. Mostly because the pastor overplayed strengths that grew into a fatal weakness.

Your personal preference in worship style is relatively insignificant, and it should take back seat to the priority of God's kingdom advancing. As pastor, you are called to serve the congregation. Start from where the congregation is, and move with community input to keep community ownership to help the church respond to the larger community needs. But because for so many of us, worship issues *are* important, differences in style may be a reason for you *not* to go to a specific ministry. Find a good match of worship styles in a congregation you are considering. However, remember you and the congregation will both change over time, so there is room for change and growth as well!

A desired quality level in worship is a norm of any congregation. In some cases the relationships are more important than quality. A musician far past his prime or with skills not comparable to those of other musicians will not be replaced, because it would hurt his feelings. Song leaders with identified limits will be left in place, and the congregation can't grow into new experiences in worship. When the norm is "everyone gets to participate," everybody gets to participate. Another congregation has a norm of quality and will use the most qualified musicians in worship. This congregation offers training and opportunities to grow toward the skill level required in public worship.

Some congregations need well-planned worship without surprises and changes. Messing with their worship is messing with their experience of God. Another congregation needs worship to be spontaneous as a proof of God's active leadership. Congregations do what they intend even when they can't articulate the reasons.

## Special Situations

There are churches in special situations that change all the normal rules. The internal dynamics of individuals and the system will override usual norms in situations of ongoing conflict and situations following clergy misconduct.

### Conflicted Congregations

Take particular notice of congregations that are conflicted. Conflicted churches aren't conflicted over a single issue, especially the issue du jour; they are conflicted with revolving manifestations. There exist fault lines, groups, or individual protagonists that will inevitably renew the conflict. The underlying issue is how the participants in conflict conduct themselves. When feelings are owned and positions are stated, the other persons are heard and valued, and this is healthy conflict. Conflict that is willing to do harm to win must be prevented. This second kind of conflict will not manifest the expected slow escalation of conflict; it will burst forth, at the same intensity level that it reached in the preceding cycle, with little if any correlation to the significance of the presenting issue.

Look at the church over a period of time. Short ministry tenures and significant fluctuations in attendance and church income are indicators of ongoing conflict. It is our observation that extended conflict will inhibit spiritual growth and leadership development. These limits will manifest themselves individually as well as corporately. Presenting issues are rarely the underlying issues in conflicted systems.

### "After" Churches

"After" churches are those churches that have experienced some form of clergy misconduct. The significance of the breach of trust on the part of the clergy is enhanced by the unique nature of the clergy role. Clergy are involved in major life events of family systems. Ministering to a family in a time of crisis, death, or trauma raises the intensity of the relationship between clergy and parishioner. Thus the betrayal of trust becomes even more devastating. Second, there is an embodiment of the divine in the clergy role that causes congregants to feel betrayed by the clergy and betrayed by God.

Because of the intensity of feelings, emotions can't be owned or discussed. The system experiences a great deal of transference of anger and assignment of blame. The system can appear calm on the surface but manifest extreme turbulence below the surface.

These churches will not be able to grant trust to incoming clergy. Nor will they likely be able to bond with the incoming pastor. Full congregational disclosure of all information about the conduct of the offending pastor will help in the short term and in the long term. It will help eliminate competing truths about what the church has experienced.[3]

Before you accept such a situation, be sure that you are informed about the unique dynamics, that you understand what the church needs to accomplish to establish health, and that you have a good support network. Count the cost for you, for your family, and for the time that will be required. These situations can extract a tremendous toll on the clergy and the clergy family.

Know that you have support for taking on a challenge with significant risk. These special situations require pastoral leadership that is measured, intentional, and consistent. Riley accepted his last pastorate with full knowledge of its history of conflict and with a priority of addressing those needs. He had the support of the judicatory even if it was without optimism. The judicatory head said, "We won't hold this against you if it doesn't work." God was gracious, and the church was able to break the power of the hidden controller by removing the person who kept the system destabilized. This cannot happen until a strong majority of the church and the leaders are ready to call individuals to account for disruptive and destructive actions.

Once again, what we are saying is to know the church and to know yourself. The better picture you have of self and new situation, the more likely the match will be satisfying to all in the long run. With adequate knowledge, even the most challenging situation may be one that you are willing, indeed feel called, to respond to, knowing that you go into it with God at your side. Our love of God and our deep desire to be faithful before God might give us a false positive when we consider serving the local church in a ministerial role.

## Applying the Principles

### A Hard Wait

John knew it was time to move. He and his wife were encouraged because they had five contacts in six months. As he prayerfully pondered these specific opportunities, John was led to turn down each church following the committees' first contact. It was tempting to pursue the sixth church and try to make it work, because that situation was the last visible opportunity. After John turned down the sixth church, his wife said, "What are you going to do now?" He responded that he was committed to wait on God for the right one. It was hard, with a lot of second guessing of his earlier decisions, but John grew in his commitment to wait on the Lord. They did wait, and the right situation did come along.

### Choosing a Different Pastoral Role

Following a successful ministry at his second church, Brennan felt it was time for a transition in ministry. He was contacted by one of the larger congregations in the state. His reaction was excitement and caution. This church had a well-earned reputation for conflict. After he prayed, pondered, and sought counsel from friends and his wife, Brennan felt he should pursue the possibility but with the intention to address the conflict. So he was called, and his ministry was one of preparing the congregation to address the conflict that was sure to come.

In Brennan's fourth year, the conflict did come, and the leaders were prepared and willing to implement the plans they had made. The intervention was successful. In the next couple of years, Brennan and his leaders discovered that the church couldn't let him change his pastoral role from change agent to pastor. During this year he came to realize the emotional drain and pain he was experiencing. He also became increasingly aware how much pain his wife and children had accumulated. It was time for a move.

## Suggestions for Your *Next Steps*

- Weigh and identify your leadership style, the type of worship, the type of community, and the special situations you are willing to consider and accept.

- What additional skills or experiences might you pursue now to prepare yourself for a new ministry context?

- Will your personal and professional needs be met in the ministry you are considering? Why or why not?

## Suggestions for *Prayer*

- Thank God for opportunities that might be put before you.

- Ask God's help as you consider possibilities put before you, asking God to help you discern what you can and cannot do.

- In each situation you might consider asking God to reveal those situations you are prepared to handle and those that might be beyond your skills and abilities. The most prestigious congregation may look good on paper, but if it requires skills you don't have, you need to ask God to help you see your limitations. Or, you might ask God to help you see what unknown skills you have and the situation you can to step into.

- Ask God to help you get wise counsel as you consider the opportunities set before you.

**NOTES**

1. John C. Larue Jr., "Forced Exits: High-Risk Churches," *Your Church* (posted 4/4/2009) www.christianitytoday.com/yc/more/specialreport/6y3072 .html (accessed March 29, 2011).

2. Marcia Barnes Bailey, *Choosing Partnership, Sharing Ministry: A Vision for New Spiritual Community* (Herndon, VA: The Alban Institute, 2007).

3. Nancy Myers Hopkins, *The Congregation Is Also a Victim* (Bethesda, MD: Alban Institute Inc., 1993), 11.

# CHAPTER 6

# Overview of the Search and Call Process

"So come, I will send you to Pharaoh to bring my people, the Israelites, out of Egypt." But Moses said to God, "Who am I that I should go to Pharaoh, and bring the Israelites out of Egypt?" (Exodus 3:10-11)

*Churches relate to one* another in two primary models. The first is the congregational or free church model, such as governs the Baptist conventions, United Church of Christ, The Christian Church—Disciples of Christ, and Church of the Brethren. In this tradition, the decision of who will be pastor of a local church rests totally and only with the local church. The second is the connectional model, such as that employed by the United Methodist, African Methodist Episcopal, and Roman Catholic Church. Here the decision of who will pastor a local church rests with the denominational leaders. Some denominations, such as Lutheran, Episcopal, and Presbyterian churches, combine the two models. Local churches have freedom to find their leaders but within certain strict boundaries set by the denomination.

The last twenty years have seen hybrids develop in all systems. Judicatories are offering autonomous congregations more and more services in the search and call process. Judicatories often serve as a source of clergy names. They offer congregations material for self-study, and increasingly they seek to facilitate matching of congregations and clergy who demonstrate compatibility. This is in addition to local and regional relationship resourcing.

Judicatories and national offices in connectional models are seeking and honoring more input from local congregations. Some systems, because of the nature of the relationship, unilaterally appoint clergy to specific churches. The judicatories and national entities describe the process as being among three partners. The three players are denomination, clergy, and local church.[1] These changes give more support to autonomous congregations and more voice to congregations in connectional relationships.

OVERVIEW OF THE SEARCH PROCESS

Ministerial vacancy occurs

Church secures the services of an interim

Search committee is formed
   1. Agrees on a process
   2. Meets with judicatory resource person

Search committee completes self-study

Search committee receives names and profiles
   1. Names submitted by members or friends of congregation
   2. Solicited by committee from trusted sources
   3. Solicitated from the judicatory

Committee reviews candidate profiles
   1. Checks references
   2. Reviews audio-visual materials submitted
   3. Conducts interviews
   4. Develops general salary and benefit terms in a draft work agreement
   5. Presents a candidate to the church

Candidate comes to the church

Vote is taken to call the candidate

New minister arrives
   1. Installation is held
   2. After six months, first evaluation of minister is conducted

# Local Church Process

## Church Step 1: Preparation

We offer a similar overview of a church process so you can have an appreciation of a committee's work. It will help you to remember that committees are potentially working with several candidates, which will lengthen their response time.

Because an individual congregation infrequently searches for pastoral leadership, they often lack experience in this important area of church life. On average, churches search for ministers about every five years. Ideally the church will identify and hold to a process by which it seeks, identifies, and calls a new minister. Denominations often have set processes to follow, and if a congregation contacts their denominational officer they will find useful resources. The Alban Institute also has resources for the local church in this endeavor. We will describe a generally typical process with particular attention given to how it intersects with the minister in transition.

Following the resignation, retirement, or termination of a pastor, the church forms a search committee as prescribed by its guiding documents. If there are internal issues such as a long preceding pastorate or internal struggles, the search committee may be delayed in formation or the church may put its process on hold. The church will grieve the loss of the former minister. It is essential that the process allows individuals and the congregation to have room in their heart for a new minister. Most congregational systems highly recommend that churches use an interim pastor, one called for a specific or undefined but brief time (one to two years) while the search committee does its work.

### THE SELF-STUDY

The first step for a local church is to enter a self-study process. This self-awareness allows the church to know the spiritual gifts and skills it needs the new minister to possess. The identification of needed skills will allow God to speak through the congregation and through the candidates to the search committee. The mantra of a search committee should be, "Is this the right one?" A skill-based search can prevent a church from being caught up in the charisma of a candidate who doesn't match the identified needs of the church. A basketball analogy can explain the validity of a skill-based search: "It doesn't matter how good a guard a person is if you really need a forward." As a candidate, you want to look for ways you connect with the materials the committee provides you. You want to see ways your skills match the skills and gifts the search committee is looking for. If they indicate that they are looking for a person who can bring growth in social outreach but your gifts are in teaching and nurturing, you might want to look elsewhere.

## PREPARE INFORMATION FOR THE CANDIDATE

The self-study not only has helped the committee understand the church, but also the documents they have collected during the study will form the basic information packet to be shared with potential pastoral candidates. The information suggested to the committee usually includes history, demographics of the church and the community in which the church is situated, an organizational chart, life of the church (programs and how those programs are run), worship expectations, theological understandings, and the vision and mission of the church. The committee will identify the expectations and needs of the congregation with respect to the spiritual gifts and the ministry skills desired in the pastor to be called. In addition, they should have some idea of the anticipated salary and benefits package they can offer a pastor.

After the development of materials describing the church, its ministries, and its understanding of the gifts and skills needed by a candidate, the search committee compiles the material to be shared with candidates. Churches may create a single document or perhaps a notebook. Often committees gather the material and place it on a website. You may not find a fully articulated job description in this material, but people should get a clear idea of the current functioning of the congregation, its history, and its hope for the future.

The kind of history you will find in a church profile differs depending upon the church. You may find a booklet from a recent anniversary event, or you may find a compilation of a church history. In considering the church's history you want to look for how people are involved in the history of the church. You also want to consider especially how the last few pastors have fared in the church. You may want to do your own historical search or contact previous pastors to see what they have to say about the church.

You might expect to see in the profile an organizational chart of the church's governance structure. This may be a chart or a descriptive page of how the church accomplishes its business.

The individual church demographics can include gender ratios, age ranges, employment categories (full-time, part-time, retired, unemployed), family make-up (single, married, married with children), and perhaps even a chart indicating income ranges. You should also expect to see information about the community the church serves.

Pages on the life of the church describe both what organizations exist within the church (e.g., a women's organization or Sunday school) and programs that are open to all which the church considers part of how it works together. You will find very different ideas of this depending on the size and composition of the community of faith, where it is in the country, and whether it is urban or rural.

You might expect to find pages that describe how the community of faith approaches worship. Do they typically use hymns or praise choruses or a combination of both? Who typically selects the songs the congregations sings? Does the church use a lot of litanies, or are they not even familiar with this word? Do they use a common lectionary for Scripture readings and sermon texts, or does the pastor or worship leader choose a Scripture based on other factors? Does the congregation read Scripture in unison, or is a single reader chosen to read aloud? Do they have a choir or a praise team? Do they have a handbell choir or a children's choir? How do children participate in worship, if at all? How often and how is communion served?

You should also expect to find some kind of statement about the church's foundational beliefs. This might be from its constitution or covenant. Each church approaches this task differently, but if you do not find such a statement somewhere, it is an important initial inquiry to make of a congregation.

One of the primary things potential candidates ought to look for in a church profile is the church's vision and mission. Both words are used today to describe the direction the church sees as most important for itself in the days ahead. Every church could engage in many ministries. Churches vary in understanding their mission or articulating their vision. As you find statements of vision and/or mission, you need to decide if that vision is one you can embrace and that you have the skills and gifts to lead the congregation toward.

### Church Step 2: Collecting Résumés and Profiles

During the development of this resource, the search committee may be receiving information from possible candidates. They may receive names from their judicatory at the end of the self-study process. Putting your profile or résumé before as many churches as possible is your goal at this point. The discernment of particular situations will come later.

Search committees generally sift through the information about candidates and determine which ones they want more information from. They will write an introductory letter, which will let potential candidates know the bare facts of the church. A cover letter will tell you in what city or town the church is located and something in general about the church. The letter is developed to ask if the person is still willing to have a conversation about being a possible candidate. If this happened in person, it would be an introduction and an invitation to sit and talk.

### Church Step 3: First Round of Discerning between Candidates

Assuming that you have replied yes and remain on the committee's list, their next step will be to send you the information they collected or direct you to the website they created. They may then ask for further information or schedule a telephone or Skype interview. They will also contact those people you have suggested to them as references. A wise committee will contact all references provided by the candidates. During the reference call, the committee representative may ask for the names of other persons who know you and your ministry. This allows the committee to gain insight beyond the three to five references you provided—so you might provide those top-choice references with other names they might suggest to the committee representative.

There are two cycles of discernment, both happening simultaneously. This provides checks and balances in the process, because both the candidate and the institution must strongly agree that this is God's direction for them. Be prepared to wait for God's answer; don't let your needs or your ambition lead you astray. Know that waiting on God and trusting God is essential in your search.

## Candidate Search Process

### Candidate Step 1: Preparation

We have already written about how to discern your gifts and skills and make the decision to at least begin consideration of a move to a different ministry. But exactly how to go about doing that is another process altogether.

Generally your first step is to prepare the information that will introduce you to a search committee or agency looking for a leader. In most cases this means building your résumé or completing your denomination's profile information or both. There is the rare occasion when a local church search committee is in touch with you, indicating that someone has suggested that you might be a possible next pastor for their church. However, even in that case, an initial response (if you are willing to consider the invitation) is to develop a résumé or complete your denomination's profile.

When developing a résumé or profile you must keep in mind the recipients of the information rather than simply thinking about your passions and skills. In other words, if you are seeking a pastorate, what will a search committee of a local church look for? Write your résumé or profile with a search committee in mind. What will they want to know about you as a potential candidate for pastor? For instance, you might enjoy playing volleyball in the church you are serving. The important thing for a search committee is that you enjoy working with the youth, not so much that you play volleyball with them. The next church may not have places to play volleyball, or their youth might prefer other activities. Lift up the general ministries you do well and avoid dealing with specifics of how they are done.

Keep in mind the kind of ministry you feel you are best suited for as you build a résumé or profile. If you are looking for a local church pastorate, say something about the preaching task and indicate your approach to the work of the church, both as you list experience and as you indicate your passion for ministry. Denominational profiles have different ways of trying to help you approach this task. Appendix A provides the list that American Baptist Personnel Services has developed for pastors to choose their ministry skill specialties. In the American Baptist system, local churches choose from the same list what they want their pastor to do. Ideally there will be the kind of match between what you want to do and what a church wants a pastor or ministry leader to do.[2]

Another part of your preparatory work is to list references. For references, find people who know you and your work well. If you can, use people you have directly worked with in ministry. Don't use persons from your current ministry as references, unless it is a very special relationship. If you do a lot of ecumenical work or sit regularly with other ministry colleagues, ask them to serve as references. Don't assume that everyone you relate to will give you a good reference. Ask persons, "I'd like to list you as a reference. If you were called for a reference on me, could you give me a positive recommendation?" If the answer is anything but an enthusiastic yes, don't use the person as a reference. A lukewarm or negative reference will sabotage your process.

At this point, be prepared to wait a minimum of two to three months for initial contacts with churches. The process of getting your name to a church that is open can easily take a month. Then there is the wait for churches to get to the résumé part of their process. It is not uncommon for churches to receive and process two or three groups of résumés. A church can take six to eighteen months or longer to complete its self-study. Check around which churches are open and searching. Don't wait for your name to be put in through the system; ask the system to put your name in.

## Candidate Step 2: Circulating Your Profile or Résumé

The first task is either writing to express interest in a pastoral position that you hear is open or receiving a letter from a committee that hears that you are a pastor they might be interested in (either because your name was given to them or your name came to the committee from the computer profile system of your denomination). We all hope for the latter, but more often than not it is the former, the pastor doing the work to find the churches that are searching for a pastor.

Denominational, nondenominational, and independent churches have a set of prevailing norms for seeking a transition in ministry. It will benefit clergy greatly in a new call to know the rules. When you have decided it is time for a transition to a new ministry, you must trigger the process. If you feel God leading you to move, it is part of being faithful to God to activate the process. Begin by preparing appropriate materials for your context. Some systems use a common résumé form, and others don't. Find out the practices of your system. If you desire to be considered by more than one system, find out the access process for any group you want to consider you.

It is the practice in many faith communities that one of the ways a committee gets names is by contact with other clergy. One pastor (sometimes a nearby neighbor or another respected clergy from far away) will be asked if he or she has any people to recommend to a search committee. If you are a member of this community, you must work not only your denominational structure but also your contact network. To network means meeting and corresponding with clergy. Get to know them. If you are looking for a new place of ministry, tell your network and ask their assistance.

It sometimes happens that clergy are contacted without action on their part. This is time to let God be God. It is possible that God has something for you that you weren't looking for. It is responsible and part of our life of faithfulness to consider these unexpected possibilities.

If you are part of a denomination, contact the appropriate denominational leaders about the fact that you are open to move. In the American Baptist system, that usually means contacting executive or area ministers, providing them a copy of the denominational profile and a description of the kind of church you are looking for. Our clergy are also urged to check the Ministry Opportunities Listing. This is a list of churches that are seeking pastors and other church ministry positions. Most denominations have such a posting, and there are other resources such as listings in Christian magazines and on websites. Wherever you find that there is a ministry opportunity that appears interesting to you, send your information to the person indicated. Remember to keep all this in prayer, and ask your family and friends who can keep confidences to keep it in prayer as well.

### Candidate Step 3: Contact from a Church

Good news! You have received the first contact from a local church. Now how will you respond?. You may want to explore via the Internet or ministry contacts to learn more information about a church to understand more fully if you see any possibility for a match. If you choose to respond positively, reply to the tone of the letter that has been sent to you; include the information the committee requires in a clear and concise way. These inquiry letters are usually sent with a qualifying time line: "If you are interested, please contact us with the following information within two weeks." You will be wise to respond in some way within the time line. If you cannot meet the deadline, correspond with them and negotiate a different deadline. If you do not want to pursue any conversation with them, respond with a thank you and your reply.

### Candidate Step 4: Discernment

If you have replied that you are willing to proceed, the next correspondence should have the information the committee has gathered in its church profile. Committees generally also ask for further information from you. They may as early as this second correspondence ask for a sermon or samples of other written material, church newsletters, or bulletins. If you are one of those who need to move, you should have a sermon taped or videotaped for you, so you can provide this information when a committee asks. It is prudent to have several sermons available so you can choose one that you feel is good for the situation to which it is being sent. There is nothing more off-putting to committees than to watch a videotaped sermon that is preached for the camera, rather than live. However, poorly taped pieces are just as detrimental. If at all possible, plan in advance and have copies made of a sermon that is delivered to a congregation and that is done well. It isn't helpful to say to a search committee, "I'll have a sermon in two weeks, after I have a chance to ask someone to record my next sermon."

In these contacts with a church, you do not know whether the committee meets regularly or not, but assume that it does. If the committee gives you deadlines, by all means at least meet them, and preferably, exceed them. If for some reason you cannot meet the deadline, tell the committee as soon as possible the circumstances that prevent you from meeting them and let them know when to expect to hear more from you. On the other side, committees are notorious for failing to communicate in a thoughtful manner with candidates. They may set a date for you, and then you may not hear from them for some time. If the deadline they set has passed and within two or three weeks you have not heard anything, it is alright to send an inquiry to ask when you might expect to hear from them.

Anticipate that committee members will check your references at some point, and be prepared to provide additional names and contact information if they ask for them. While the church does a first round of discernment, you have to provide appropriate responses, keep the process always in prayer, and be prepared. At this time, prepare for interviews when they happen.

At this point, you should be looking for a match in the skills you have and the church expresses a need for. Further, consider the community and ministry from as many perspectives as you can. You are looking for a sense of "this could work." You don't have all of the information you will gain in an interview process. If you discover any reasons you could not consider this situation, tell the committee as soon as possible. This will help you and them not to invest time and energy considering a possibility that cannot happen.

For further reflection we recommend *The Unauthorized Guide to Choosing a Church* by Carmen Renee Berry.

## Applying the Principles

### What Is Expected?

Maria has decided it is time to make a transition in ministry. She begins to think about what will be expected of her in the search and call process. It occurs to her that she doesn't know what materials or response a new ministry will expect of her. She realizes that she doesn't understand what a ministry does to call its next person. Maria calls her judicatory resource to have her explain the church side of the search and call process.

### It's in the Details

After five years at her second church, Gayle came to the prayerful conclusion that it was time for her to look for another ministry opportunity. Five churches had contacted her in the first year she circulated her résumé. The churches were all excited in their initial contact with her, but none of them interviewed her or included her in their final group. She asked one of the chairpersons she felt she had connected with why the church didn't consider her further. The committee chair told Gayle that one of her primary references did not express confidence in her skills or potential to grow. Reluctantly the committee chair told her which reference was not affirming her. Gayle remembered that she had asked the person to be a reference but had failed to ask this pastor if he would be able to give her a good reference. She contacted another person to replace the previous person. This time she asked, "Will you be able to give me a good reference?" After receiving a positive response, Gayle removed the original reference and added the person who would affirm her. In the next six months, she was contacted, interviewed, and called by a congregation.

## Suggestions for Your *Next Steps*

- Where are you in the search and call process?
- What do you need to do to prepare for ministry what may be next for you?

## Suggestions for *Prayer*

- Thank God for your current ministry.
- Ask God to prepare you for the process at hand.
- Ask for God's leading as you go through each step of the process.
- Ask God for guidance as you seek discernment at each step of the process.

### NOTES

1. La Crosse Area Synod, ELCA, "Call Process for Calling a Pastor" (June 4, 2009) http://www.lacrosseareasynod.org/wp-content/uploads/callpstr.pdf (accessed March 29, 2011).

2. Mary Mild, ed., *Calling an American Baptist Pastor* (Valley Forge, PA: National Ministries, 2004), 63–64.

# CHAPTER 7
# The Interview Process

Now who will harm you if you are eager to do what is good? . . . Do not fear what they fear, and do not be intimidated, but in your hearts sanctify Christ as Lord. Always be ready to make your defense to anyone who demands from you an accounting for the hope that is in you; yet do it with gentleness and reverence. (1 Peter 3:13-16a)

*If a search committee is open* to further conversation, it is generally the next step that an interview will be set up. A first interview may be by phone. Remember that this is an interview and not a seminary test. If you haven't done work interviews in a while, you might gather a small group of friends, share the materials you have, and ask them to put you through a mock interview.

The interview is sometimes a complex thing. There usually are several interviews before the whole process is complete. The idea in an interview is both for the committee to get a better idea of you and for you to get a better idea of the church. Pick and choose which questions are most important to you. There may well be questions that are more important for you. If you have a particular concern, let's say, building homes with Habitat for Humanity, you may need to ask specifically how this service might be received by the church. You may also find that questions posed to you at a first interview or answers you received from questions you asked at the first interview may bring up questions or concerns in subsequent interviews.

## The Purpose of the Interview

The interview process is a time to examine values, attitudes, temperaments, hopes and dreams for the future, faith journeys, and theological concepts. These and other discussion points will help all parties to discern if compatibility exists. The interview is the time to get acquainted with one another and to engage in mutual sharing of facts concerning you and the church or other employing organization. As a candidate, go to the interview with your own list of questions. Let the search committee ask questions first, however. What they ask may answer some of your questions.

In the interview you are seeking an answer, but you can also learn a great deal about the nature of the congregation or organization. If just one person conducts the entire interview, there may be real limits on shared leadership in congregational life. If a group interviews you, note who is represented. Are both men and women present, and are they given equal voice in the discussion? Are church leaders and nonleaders represented? Is there any diversity of culture, race, or generation among the interviewers if there is in the organization? Do the members seem homogenous in terms of theology, demographics, and perspective on the organization and the position to be filled? The answers to these questions (all unspoken) may communicate a great deal about the church or organization you are considering.

## The Interview with the Search Committee

After an interview is scheduled but before you talk with the search committee, you will find it beneficial to talk with some other folks about the church or organization—folks who are in a position to know about the ministry and its people. Their information will be critical because it will be more objective and provide a longer perspective than your first impressions can offer. This background information can inform your interview with the search committee.

In the case of a church ministry, contact the denominational person who works most closely with the congregation. This person should be able to give you a long view of church life and its nature. Also contact the previous pastor, who may or may not be objective but who will have some significant insights and experiences to share. If you know other pastors in the area of the church you are considering, initiating a conversation with them may also be helpful to you.

In other ministry positions, be sure to visit the organizational website to find out what the organization says about itself. Contact local churches, agencies, or businesses that may interact with the organization, and find out how the organization is viewed in the community. If the ministry is a member of or sponsored by a larger organization or affinity group, contact individuals from that other organization or group. If possible, have conversations with former or current employees, both clergy and laity, about their experiences with the ministry.

This chapter provides a reasonable overview of the content that pastoral search committees may cover when interviewing a candidate. If you are interviewing for a ministry position outside the parish setting, you may also expect an interview that will cover a comparable range of questions and issues. Prepare yourself for the interview by drafting responses to the questions provided in this book and in others that may be more specific to your new ministry setting, be it corporate, nonprofit, or church-related. In preparation and in the interview itself, pay attention to the questions—and remember that any interview is a conversation between two or more parties, some or all of whom will be laity. On one occasion, Riley responded to a question from a search committee member with a five-minute answer. After he finished, his wife, who was participating in the interview with him, said, "That was a yes or no question, Riley."

An initial interview may be conducted by phone or Skype. If so, be prepared for that interview as well. If you are using an electronic medium, test the connections prior to the meeting. If it is a medium that uses video, make sure that what the committee can see is what you want them to see (your study, if it is clean and neat, or a plain wall or wall of books; remember everything at this point can make an impression). Whether the interview is by phone or other electronic medium, be sure you can be someplace where you will not be interrupted unnecessarily during the interview. As you wait for the contact call or time to come, pray and prepare yourself as though you were seeing the committee face to face.

Much of the effectiveness of the interview will depend on the preparation of the committee and of you. Ideally you will find that the committee has adhered to the following suggestions, but regardless of their preparation, you as a candidate must be focused and ready to participate.

You should review the materials you have been given and prepare a list of questions for the committee. Occasionally committees are not prepared to interview, and you may want to be prepared to prompt them with questions you anticipated they would ask. You may want to talk about their relationship with the denomination or their former pastors. You may want to consider toward the end of the interview asking them what their process will be from this point on. Before you agree to be their candidate for pastor, you should have at least an introductory conversation about salary and benefits.

You might consider some of the following questions, if they are not answered in the profile or if they need clarification:

LEADERSHIP EXPECTATIONS

- How does your church expect the pastor to take leadership?
- To what extent does the church expect the pastor to share leadership?
- How are the church's ideas and plans conceived and implemented?
- How are decisions made in the church? How does the church think decisions ought to be made?

COMMUNICATION AND CONFLICT

- How do leaders communicate with the church—formally or informally, in writing or verbally from pulpit or lectern?
- How does the church make use of conflict and confrontation?

TRADITION AND INNOVATION

- How has the church been influenced by history and tradition?
- How does the church use contemporary ideas and trends?

THEOLOGY AND SOCIAL JUSTICE

- What is the church's approach to social issues?
- Which social justice issues, if any, are of particular interest to the congregation?
- How does the church deal with ethical dilemmas and decisions?

COMMUNITY INTERACTION

- How and how often is the church involved in community affairs?
- How does the church interact with the community?
- In what specific ways does this interaction take place?

DENOMINATIONAL RELATIONSHIP

- How does the church relate to the denomination?
- To what extent are church members aware of the congregation's denominational identity?
- Does the church give regularly to denominational offerings?
- What percentage of giving goes toward denominational mission? What percentage of giving goes toward all missions?

## Face-to-Face Interviews

The church or organization should be responsible for all expenses related to hosting you (and your spouse, if appropriate) for the interview. You may expect those expenses to include transportation (airfare or mileage allowance per current IRS guidelines), housing, and meals. Be sure to request in advance that a check for these expenses be available to you before leaving the interview.

You should receive written confirmation that provides all the details of the interview, including the date, time, and exact location of the interview, travel directions, expense arrangements, and schedule of events. Even if you have discussed these details by telephone, it is important that the information be verified in written form; either an email or a letter will suffice. It is desirable to have this information at least a week in advance of the scheduled interview. The week will allow for any snags to be worked out between the candidate and the search committee chair.

If you are married and especially if you are considering parish ministry, we recommend that your spouse be involved in the interview. As the candidate, it is your information that the committee is seeking, but your spouse's reactions will be a part of the family decision. You may have to negotiate your spouse's participation with the committee; it would be worth your while to pay for your spouse's travel if expense is a consideration.

The time allotted for the interview should be sufficient to allow for comprehensive discussion—preferably two to three hours if at all possible. If your spouse is invited, then the interview process should include additional time for spousal participation.

Plan your travel to allow time to refresh yourself before the interview. If the committee's proposed schedule includes a tour of the facility and the community and meeting with other staff or key members, request an extra hour or two between those activities and the interview. Use that time to freshen up and even take a quick nap!

The committee should have an informal agenda for the interview. Ideally they will also determine in advance who will cover which topics so that the entire committee participates in the interview. The committee may also be watching closely to see how you respond to different questioners—to women versus men, to people of a different race or generation, to assertive personalities versus tentative ones. Committee questions should encompass areas of particular concern as well as the professional specialties highlighted by the congregation or organization.

The search committee will determine the interview agenda—but they should not dominate it. Make sure that the agenda gives you time to explore your questions and concerns. As noted above, prepare your questions in advance. Then alert the committee chair before the interview begins so that the agenda may be adjusted as needed.

Ideally the interview will be conducted in a location where interruptions will be few to none and where the setting promotes a relaxed friendliness. This may be at the church or place of business, in a committee member's home, or in a private room at a restaurant. If you are given an option, choose one of these, but do your best to avoid having the interview in a public place like a restaurant. If you do not have a choice, make the best of it; the committee may be checking to see how you handle less than the best situations.

## Suggested Content for Interviews

Because good search committees will attempt to keep their interviews as similar as possible to provide a sound basis for comparison, you may expect some or all of these formulaic questions.

- Describe your salvation experience
- Describe your call to ministry
- Describe your understanding of local church ministry
- Describe your gifts for ministry
- What are you looking for in the church you hope to serve?
- What do you need to know about us?

Effective church search committees will have worked with the congregation and leaders to identify ministry priorities—the areas of church life that the church feels are most important and where leadership is most desired. You may expect several questions that address those priorities and explore your passion for or commitment to those issues.

If the search committee focuses on theological or doctrinal issues, that may be a red flag indicating one or more issues that should concern a minister in transition. The organization may be focused on matters of orthodoxy over ministry. After you answer their direct question, you may want to explore with them what brings this question to the forefront in an interview. Congregations in general are more relational than theological. However, proceed with some caution, because the committee may have been burned by theological issues in prior contacts. That is why it might be helpful to enter into dialogue over issues that are more about orthodoxy than ministry.

The core ministry skills such as preaching, teaching, and pastoral care are built on spiritual gifts. The skills we demonstrate are a combination of natural talents, spiritual gifts, education, experience, and ministry needs. Life experience and experiences outside ministry are often building blocks of our skills in ministry. Looking back over our lives, we each can identify how God prepared us for ministries that lay ahead. Serving as a police chaplain exposed Riley to dealing with a wide variety of people, including the strong-willed, aggressive, and mentally unbalanced. The opportunity to serve on a denominational governing board gave Riley significant insight into how the denominational system worked.

An interview with a search committee is the best opportunity for them to discover who you are and what gifts and skills you bring to ministry. This same interview is the best time for you to discover who the church is and what it seeks in its next minister. Go to the interview prepared with both questions about the ministry and answers to their questions.

Always remember that the interview process is a two-way street, a time for a committee to hear about you and a time for you to learn about the organization you may be called to serve. The questions a committee asks you can give you insight into the organization. The questions you ask of the committee will give them insight into you.

You need to be prepared for interviews. If it has been awhile since you have participated in interviews or if you have felt that interviews have not gone well, we recommend that you ask two or three trusted friends who care about you and your future to conduct a mock interview. Ask your friends to pretend that they are on a search committee like the one you are going to participate in. Respond to their questions as you would in an interview, and try out your questions on them, even if they, unlike the real committee members, are not able to answer them.

You can have conversation about your responses after going though all the questions or as you answer each question. The assessment or feedback is the important part of this mock interview, and it can help a lot in preparation. Remember the important reason for the mock interview is the feedback. Listen well, and take the feedback to heart as you go to the real interview. These same friends can be prayer partners for you during the real interview.

God continues the work of discernment during interviews, and we want to be prepared. Good interviews are in large part due to good homework. One hopes that committees will do their part, but whether or not they do, you will be wise to be prepared, remembering all the time to trust God.

## Coming Together: Making a Call

If you remain in contention after the reference checks and a face-to-face interview, a preaching opportunity will likely be scheduled. In some cases (this practice is more rare than it once was), a search committee or some members of it may come to your current church to hear you preach. In the event that you work with a committee that might want to skip this step, encourage them to see that it would be helpful for you as well as them.

During the weekend when you usually go to a nearby church to speak, arrange to visit the community to which you may be called. Although you ought not to go into the prospective church during services, you can see the building at some time when members are not present. You can get a feel for the community. You can even check out properties if you need to rent or purchase your own home in the area. Neutral pulpits can usually be scheduled with the help of judicatory leaders. If the church you are considering is not a part of a denomination, then you might have to help them approach an appropriate neighboring church (a town away might be the best case, rather than a place just down the street). Experience has demonstrated it is a better experience for all involved to hear candidates preach in a neutral pulpit. This is done by making arrangements with a sister church that is a responsible distance from both the candidate and the congregation.

Gather information from the church, situation, ministry needs, and work agreement. Seek to discern if the search committee is communicating reality or a desired state. Compare their reality with their desires to see if there is a disconnect. An example of a disconnect would be if the committee describes the church as committed to growth, but there have been few or no additions in the last couple of years. After full discussion, if you are prepared to accept a strong call from the church, agree to a candidating weekend. Prior to the candidating weekend and in cooperation with the search committee, develop a time line if you were to be called of when your resignation would be presented, when you would move to new field, and your start date.

## The Candidating Weekend

Before you agree to candidate at a church, you and the search committee need to have a conversation about compensation, benefits, and expenses. Although everything may feel right, when you go to a church to candidate you need to be ready to say yes if the church extends a strong call (that is, the votes are strong enough that you are comfortable in saying yes; a 90 percent or higher vote tally). Refuse to candidate with a church until you are clear what the salary range may be. It is particularly difficult for a church to go through the actions of having a pastoral candidate and have that candidate refuse a strong call. That puts a pastor's reputation on the line as well as the church's. Although it is inappropriate to have the compensation conversation too early, it is disastrous to have the compensation conversation too late, so that the pastor refuses the call because the church is not offering enough money for the pastor to live.

We want to offer two words of caution here. First, we have written in such a way to assume that search committees will select only one candidate. That is always our recommendation. However, there are churches that believe they need to provide several candidates to a church. Our experience is that this sets up both candidates and churches for failure. We strongly advise the potential pastor to decline to candidate in these kinds of situations. Multiple candidates most often end up in split churches. A search committee should be representative enough of the church that if they are in agreement, the candidating process should result in a strong call.

The second word of caution is the assumption that the committee is in agreement. It is appropriate to ask a committee if they are in complete agreement that you are the person they want to put forward to the church. You want a committee to be unanimous about your name as the pastor. We would discourage accepting an invitation to candidate from a committee that is divided about the decision. Often a church will vote the same way a committee is divided, so if the call is from a committee of five members, only four of whom agree you are the person, the vote is likely to be only 80 percent, which means that 20 percent of the congregation will have strong doubts about your leadership before you even begin. Committees are encouraged to be in one accord on this decision, and you as a candidate should feel free to ask if this is the case.

During a candidating weekend you should be exposed to as many people in the congregation as possible. You should expect to meet people in a variety of settings. You will meet with committees and groups, around meals, in question-and-answer sessions, and in worship. The church will vote at a time and in a manner consistent with its guiding documents or precedents.

## Decision Making, Call, and Installation

Throughout the process, set aside time for consideration of a specific church and its material. Have a time of prayer and Scripture reading to prepare. Remind yourself of your gifts and skills. Review the kind of church and context you are seeking. Read all the material from the church. Look at the pictures and video. Get a mind and heart around this situation. You might invite others into this time of prayer with you. If you are married, we especially encourage you to share all information with your spouse and invite him or her to pray with you. At the end of this time of prayer, share with those you've asked to join you what your plans are.

On another day, have a time of prayer and Scripture reading to prepare. Again, you may invite others to join you, and we recommend that if you are married that you include your spouse as much as possible in the process. Reread all the material from the church. Look at the pictures and video. Get a mind and heart around this situation. Consider the positive and negative aspects that come to mind. Make notes for your future use. After reviewing all the material assign a label to this situation: yes, maybe, or not this one.

One final time, have a time of prayer and Scripture reading to prepare. Read all the material from the church. Look at the pictures and video. Get a mind and heart around this situation. After reviewing the material and your notes, make sure you agree with the label you previously assigned: yes, maybe, or not this one. Your view may shift.

Whatever you decision is, walk with that opinion for a few days. If your judgment is the same after this walk, act on it. Contact the church and give it your yes or no regarding continuing the process. As you move forward, new information and new impressions will continue to present. If the further interaction with the church is consistent with your initial judgment, continue. Be aware that the pieces have to fit throughout the process. A deal breaker may occur at any time; don't overlook something later in the process that would have discouraged you early. This won't be a data decision; it will be a faith decision. The call ultimately is from God, not the church or agency, so prepare and make your decision on that basis: Is this where you believe God would have you serve?

The results of the vote taken after a candidating weekend (either immediately after or in the very near team) are usually communicated to you as candidate and the congregation. A specified time is allowed for you as the candidate to communicate your acceptance or rejection of the call. Communication usually continues through the search committee to announce to the congregation, including when you will begin your ministry with them.

It is a common practice to have a service of installation. This service memorializes the beginning of a new minister and a new phase of the ministry of the church. Such a service allows minister and congregants to renew their commitment to Christ and his church. The installation is generally planned with the pastor and church at a time when the community can participate to welcome the pastor to the community and the congregation. It is wise to plan a six-month evaluation of ministry; this provides for early course corrections and a baseline for future evaluations.

If you are passed over for consideration, it is alright to ask a committee why they chose not to consider you. You can find out what is happening only by asking churches that passed on you their reasons for passing you. You are demonstrating that you are willing to learn, and most committees will share their observations with you.

## Search Process Ethics

Clergy will have a shorter contact-consideration-decision cycle than churches do, but usually both clergy and committees will have several. Because you have initiated the process out of a sense of faithfulness to God, respond promptly as part of that same faithfulness. Commit the time and energy to participate and respond. Churches have contacted you out of their sense of faithful inquiry; please honor that. It is not easy to say no, so you might want to prepare a template letter that you can use to respond. Prayerfully decide if a particular situation is one you should pursue. Either yes or no can be the correct answer, but not answering is disrespectful to the Body of Christ.

One of the first things to note is that one should make final determinations of situations one at a time. This one-at-a-time scenario is at the stage of deciding whether or not to be a final candidate. Prior to that, your decisions are about information gathering for both parties. Once you have been invited to be the final candidate, be disciplined and focus on one at a time.

Search committees of local churches may be willing to be second on a list, but if they are, they need to know this is happening. Generally it is better for a person to consider and have conversations with people one at a time. You can always tell them that you will keep them informed in the possibility that you may be available, but once you start serious conversations with one committee or ministry, it is not fair to start conversations with another.

An important thing about contacting a church is to contact the person that the resource you consulted (website, a listing, friends) tells you to contact. If it is a regional staff person, do not go around that person and directly to the church. If it is someone on the search committee, use the address (email or postal service) that the person gives. Take your clues from the church. If they ask you to email, do so; if they ask you to use the postal service, do so. If email addresses are provided, it is fine to use that resource. Promptly provide the materials a contacting church may request. As you receive material from a church, evaluate the material prayerfully and thoroughly.

The search and call process is a dance that sometimes can make us feel out of step. Often it feels like one of those dances that begins slowly, builds to a frenzy, and then ends well with thanksgiving. Even in this situation, the axiom is true: "Trust the process." It is helpful to have a friend or two who is aware that you are in the process. Share your frustrations and joys along the way, but also know that you will need a fair amount of patience. The control is not in your hands, and you must trust that others are doing their part. Be ready to answer questions. Put grace first along the way, and you are more likely to enjoy the dance than if you build your own stress when you cannot control how fast things may move.

The interview with a search committee is a mutual learning experience. It is best not to oversell ourselves, because then we have to live up to our hype. An interview isn't complete until both parties have answered all their questions. Winning over a search committee is not the purpose of an interview; discerning the ministry expectations and gaining a sense of God's leading is.

## Applying the Principles

### Preparation

Grace is an extrovert in her work and an introvert in her private life. She is intelligent, poised, and polished. Surprises aren't fun to Grace; she does her best work and is most comfortable with preparation. The idea of preparing for an interview is natural. She will rehearse the coming event by framing both questions and answers.

On some occasions she takes a notepad with key words from her preparation time. She has an interview in the near future with a search committee. She is thinking about arranging with one of her friends to have a mock interview.

### And More Preparation

Brennan is an extrovert with good conversation and people skills. He too has an interview with a prospective employer. In his last interview, he felt his responses rambled. He is thinking about doing more preparation this time. He feels it will be better for him to know more about the company to make sure he can connect his skills from his local church ministry. Brennan has a friend who heads up the human relations department for a midsize company. He is going to have lunch with this friend to find out what employers are looking for and how he can best present his skills from ministry and the various jobs he held while in school.

### Honesty Is the Best Policy

John had two letters of inquiry that came within days of each other. Since it was early in the conversations and initially the two opportunities looked equally good, John replied to both that he was interested in further conversation and carefully answered their initial questions. One church responded within two weeks, with a link to the church profile on their website. The church intrigued John, but he wasn't sure whether he was the one to serve this particular congregation. John consulted with his wife, Cheryl, about the situation. After a week, he responded positively and included the additional materials they asked for. It was another two weeks before he heard from the second church with their profile information. In this instance he sensed an immediate fit of vision and ministry. After again consulting with his spouse, he wrote back to them with the additional material they requested.

When the first church responded to him a couple of weeks later asking for an interview, he put them off for a day or two. During that time he contacted the second church, asking what their process was going to be. They reported that they were still gathering data and would be for at least two weeks longer. He reported that another church had requested an interview but that he was much more interested in this particular situation. They assured him that they were pleased with what they saw and that he would be on their interview list. John decided to take the risk and tell the first church that he had decided to withdraw from their search. In time, the second church did call him.

## Two at a Time

Like John, Laura eventually received letters of inquiry from two churches just days apart. And like John, Laura responded to both that she was interested in a conversation. Both churches met the criteria she and her husband, Dennis, had for an urban situation, but like John, Laura felt more drawn to one church over the other when she received their profile information. However, Grace Church, which had inspired more questions than clarity when she first read the information, contacted her first for an interview. Laura agreed to a date. Before that interview occurred, Hope Church contacted her, also requesting an interview. Laura asked herself if it was right to be interviewing with two churches at the same time, but ultimately concluded it was acceptable because neither she nor the churches had identified her as a final candidate. She made arrangements for the interview at Hope as well.

At the interview with Grace Church, Laura and Dennis had a great time. Many of her questions were clarified, and she felt that there was more of a fit than she had originally thought. At the end of the interview, she asked them what their next steps were. They would be interviewing two other candidates and would contact her in about a month about setting a date to preach in a neutral pulpit.

Subsequently Laura and Dennis went to Hope Church for an interview. She was as impressed with this church as she had initially felt. They not only clarified her few questions but also asked her good questions. She was ready to accept, if they would call her. Again, Laura asked what the committee's process was going to be. They expected to make their decision about whom to call for a neutral pulpit in about a month's time.

When Grace Church followed up first, that put Laura in a dilemma. She disclosed to them that she was also in conversation with another pulpit committee and did not want to lead them on. She decided to trust God in what she was feeling and told the Grace committee to go ahead with their other candidate. If, after hearing that person, they felt that they still needed to hear her, she would reconsider. (She knew she would hear from Hope Church by that time.) Ultimately, she heard from the Hope Church also and preached at a neutral pulpit. Laura was called as pastor of Hope Church, and the move worked well for her and her spouse.

## Suggestions for Your *Next Steps*

- What questions are you prepared to answer in an interview?
- What questions do you need answered by a committee?

## Suggestions for *Prayer*

- Ask God for a strong sense of what you need to share about your ministry and yourself.
- Ask God to grant a clear understanding of what you need to know about this ministry and its priorities.
- If you are facing an interview, thank God for the committee and their work. Ask God to give you wisdom, clear thinking, and careful use of your mouth.

# CHAPTER 8
# Getting to the Details

"Since we have heard that certain persons who have gone out from us, though with no instructions from us, have said things to disturb you and have unsettled your minds, we have decided unanimously to choose representatives and send them to you, along with our beloved Barnabas and Paul. . . . For it has seemed good to the Holy Spirit and to us to impose on you no further burden than these essentials. . . ." (Acts 15:24-25,28)

*God is a part* of our work together; we've said this over and over. The work of Paul and Barnabas was easier because they had a clear task set before them because of the letter of the Jerusalem Council. And this chapter is going to look at job descriptions, which can often be seen as mundane and all about business. We don't want to forget, though, that God is a part of the process and that includes the development of and agreement to a job description. Be in prayer over the job description, just as you are about the rest of the materials and opportunities in consideration of a new ministry.

The preliminary work of a local church search committee is to get to know the church, its past, it current situation, and its vision for the future. One of the purposes for this work is to determine what it is they want a pastor to be doing within their community of faith for the foreseeable future. As such, their work can eventually be developed into a job description. That does not mean you will immediately find a document with a job description in the materials you receive from a search committee. At some point, however, you want to be sure that an appropriate agreement is in place. It will help you in your first months of ministry especially and will help the search committee and the church as they understand your work among them.

## Job Description

The most common mistake made by ministers in the search and call process is accepting a position without a clear job description in place. If the calling institution has not developed a job description, make the development of a job description a condition of the call to be accomplished in the first sixty days.

As professional church leaders, we must know what the job is if we hope to succeed. Without a job description agreed upon by the institution, every church participant plus the minister has a job description in mind. Without a job description, persons and groups, according to their own expectations, will evaluate you. It is impossible to satisfy multiple sets of expectations. A job description will make it easier to identify the parameters of the expectations.

A job description serves to clarify expectations and priorities. A functional job description is clear statement of what is expected of the minister. It will be reasonable, accomplishable, and measurable. The items identified in the scope of ministry should be prioritized so the individual will be able to focus energy. This document needs to state clearly whom the clergy supervises and to whom the clergy is primarily accountable. The agreed-upon job description should be informed by Scripture, the church constitution, and working ministry models. The church needs to develop one set of expectations to meet the needs of the largest part of its ministry and its membership that is possible.

The job description will serve as your primary evaluation instrument in the future. After all, ministers should be evaluated on the basis of what they were called to do. This will keep evaluation focused on the agreed-upon responsibilities. It will also serve as an instrument of protection. Floating priorities and personal agendas can be minimized. The job description can provide protection for minister and governing body from bullies in the congregation. We suggest that the minister ask for an evaluation in about six months. This offers an opportunity for early correction and establishes a baseline for comparison of future evaluations.

Working with no job description is like living in a house with no doors. There is no meaningful security, and you are exposed to every wind that blows through the congregation. Do not believe that having no job description will allow you to implement your personal priorities. All of the other players have their own priorities, which are as valid to them as yours is to you. And together they have more power and influence than you do.

## Work Agreement

"The laborer deserves to be paid" (Luke 10:7). In the process of call, sooner or later, usually later rather than sooner, the issue of remuneration comes up. On the one hand, it is important for you, the minister, to know your expectations and needs. On the other hand, you may need to be prepared to help a church or agency develop an appropriate package for a minister. The Internal Revenue Service (IRS) allows certain benefits for a minister, and the better you know them, the better you may be able to negotiate an appropriate package for you and your family.

If the committee doesn't make this part of some discussion, approach the chair and ask when they intend to address the issue. The logical place in the process would be following the interview and the preaching in a neutral pulpit. Don't accept the trial weekend until you and the committee have finished these negotiations and both parties have agreed in writing. This agreement must address all of the issues of significance to both parties. It is a violation of reasonable clergy ethics to receive a call and then try to negotiate with the church from that "strength of call" position.

Because churches and clergy are often timid about talking about money and details, this is an important point. There are often uncomfortable feelings on both the clergy side and the church or agency side. Clergy are often not aware that it can be as uncomfortable for the church or agency to discuss remuneration as it is for the clergy. Clergy therefore need to be well prepared for the discussion.

You need to know your needs, what benefits you can ask for and expect, and the IRS regulations so that you do not have problems down the line. This book is not about strange clergy tax laws, so we recommend that if you do not know them, you contact a knowledgeable accountant or judicatory agency that is familiar with the laws. The suggestions we offer are what we know to be in place at the time of the writing, but we urge you to check things out before you make any big changes.

## Salary and Housing

Reasonable expectations for salary, housing, and benefits from a particular church or in many other not-for-profit agencies are between 35 and 55 percent of the total income. This range of salary and benefits holds true for multiple-staff congregations as well; total salaries and benefits are between 35 and 55 percent of the total expenses of the organization. For associates with full education and experience, 80 percent of the senior pastor's salary is a reasonable level to attain. If the total clergy salary budget is more than 55 percent of the church income, two things will likely happen. One, the church won't have enough income available to conduct the rest of its ministry. Building repairs may become crises, and tension will permeate the life of the congregation. Two, every time the ministers talk about stewardship, people will hear it as asking for money for the pastors, because six cents of every dime already go to the clergy. The best way to advocate for a raise in pastoral income is to raise the income of the church or agency.

### Cash Salary

It is helpful to separate salary and housing from other benefits for clergy. However, you can legally increase take-home pay by putting reasonable amounts of salary in tax-free expense categories. These include but are not limited to convention expenses, continuing education expenses, travel expenses (including mileage for doing church business), books, periodicals, resources, and hospitality expenses for church-related matters. This is implementation of tax law, not abuse of it. Be sure to use reputable resources to guide your decision making. The church must approve in business meeting these designations at the beginning of each year for them to be valid, and you will need to provide receipts to get the money, but it will be tax-free.

A significant difference in perspective keeps clergy and lay leaders on different pages when they discuss salary. If you ask lay folks how much the clergy make, they will add up everything that goes to the clergy: salary, housing, medical benefits, and retirement benefits, as well as the expense benefits mentioned above. Pastors, like most of the laity, will look at their salary as the money that is paid directly to them. It is helpful to talk about compensation (housing, utilities, salary, and benefits) to help both the congregation and you to understand the realities of what you have to live on. Unless lay persons are in management or own a business, they don't have a complete view of employee cost. It is critical for you as clergy to help the church compare apples to apples.

In most cases, small churches of the family or pastoral type are unlikely to provide salary and benefits sufficient to support a family—not without a second income from one or both spouses. Be aware of this limitation when you consider a ministry placement, and don't assume that after a year or so, you'll renegotiate for a higher salary. Ask for what you need from the outset, being aware of the limitations and possibilities of the situation, and don't allow piety, timidity, or anxiety cause you to settle for less. Ministry transition is difficult enough without adding financial hardship or quiet resentment about being underpaid and overworked to the stress. If God is calling you to a ministry where the salary package is insufficient to meet the needs of you and your family, then you need to be aware and prepared to seek other sources of revenue, whether through a bivocational contract (see chapter 3) or through a spouse's income.

As a candidate, you need to realize that it is suggested that the church approve a salary package for the search committee to work within. Churches are best served to build in some flexibility; most often it is a range of $4,000 or so. That range is intended to address training, experience, and need. If the church preapproves a salary package, it provides guidance to the committee. Further, it will keep the call decision focused on "Is this the right one?" rather than "Do I want to pay this much for this candidate?" As a candidate, you may have some negotiating room, but you have to ask.

Be sure that you ask for and receive the full contribution of the church to your retirement. A full contribution is the same dollars or percent of salary the church has given in the past or the recommended contribution of the retirement plan you are in. There is an alarming trend of pastors and churches underfunding a full contribution to retirement. This provides a short-term savings for the church but has long-term negative impact on your retirement income. Don't do something in your life that you would not recommend to a member of your congregation. Partially funding a retirement plan gives a church an unrealistic understanding of the real cost of funding ministry.

When considering financial issues, be sure to do a cost-of-living comparison between where you are and where you might go. There are a number of resources on the Internet that can help. Be sure to choose an informed source such as Bankrate.com, the US Census Bureau, or colleges and universities. Salary information must be considered in context. We must make informed decisions in regard to salary and benefits, because we live in an unforgiving economic climate. Thoroughly discuss all of the items regarding your call before coming as the candidate. If the congregation does not offer to create a statement of agreement (free download at www.judsonpress.com), suggest to the search committee that it is necessary. A friend recently made a transition in which the search committee said, "We will take care of you financially." This friend knew better. He didn't come to an agreement before the candidating weekend, nor did he re-engage the search committee when he found out the salary. When considering your compensation package, consider the information in the following sections.

There are several things to remember when you consider a transition from paid ministry to a secular setting. First, you will be in a different tax environment regarding housing cost. You will no longer be able to have housing cost in a tax-free category. A piece of good news is that you won't have to pay Social Security and Medicare tax, because you will not be self-employed. Second, you probably will not receive reimbursement for the cost of operating your car.

## Parsonage

Some churches have parsonages that are offered to clergy as part of their compensation. This may be the largest asset the church owns besides the church building. A church cannot sell its parsonage and make enough off the principal to pay a housing allowance. Parsonages present advantages and disadvantages to both the congregation and the minister. Advantages to the congregation are a fixed cost and asset appreciation. Disadvantages to the congregation are purchase price, maintenance and improvements, and congregational energy to oversee the property.

For the pastor, a parsonage presents the advantage of living rent-free in a property where maintenance and upkeep are someone else's responsibility. The disadvantage, of course, is that at some point, clergy will likely want to accumulate equity in a home for their future. An equity agreement can maximize benefits to both parties.

The premise of the equity allowance is to allow both the church and the minister to participate in the benefits of church-owned housing. The church continues to own and operate the housing unit with a cost of the original purchase price and a relatively small payment to the employee. The church continues to benefit from the increase in the value of the house and from not having the cash outflow of housing payments in the minister's compensation package. The minister gets to share in the increasing value of the church-owned home and build toward a cash down payment for future housing needs. The agreement as presented also has a forced savings component on the part of the employee. The church contribution is conditional upon the participation of the employee. Please have a legal representative review this suggested agreement.

The _____Church of _____ will contribute the sum of $500 [you choose the figure] per year in equal semiannual (quarterly) contributions to the equity allowance account, and <u>Employee</u> will contribute the sum of $500 [you choose the figure] per year in equal semiannual (quarterly) contributions to the equity allowance account. The equity allowance account will be established at any financial institution in the name of <u>Employee</u> and <u>Church</u> of _____. The account will require two signatures for removal of money. <u>Employee</u> will determine the type of investment used for the account and the institution.

This money and the interest earned will be available to <u>Employee</u> or his/her estate upon the termination of his employment at <u>Church</u>. In the event of a family emergency <u>Employee</u> may appeal to the then current Finance Committee of <u>Church</u> seeking release of the funds accumulated by this agreement. It is understood that this contribution by <u>Church</u> will be taxable income for <u>Employee</u>.

## *Housing Allowance*

The financial condition of the congregation, community size, and housing availability are the determining variables in choosing to receive a housing allowance. The advantages of a housing allowance to a minister are accumulation of cash at sale and a sense of "my family's house." If the community is not large enough to provide a healthy market for homes, clergy will be at a significant disadvantage when buying or selling a home. Sufficient homes of the type desired are another key factor. Keep in mind that if you own your home and move to a new location, you might get the privilege of making two house payments for a time. The disadvantage of a housing allowance to a minister could arise if the minister doesn't have money for a down payment. Finally, the responsibility for upkeep and improvements could prove to be a disadvantage.

A utilities allowance should cover the actual cost of electricity, gas, water, and sewer. Consult with your tax professional to clarify what can and cannot be included in a utility allowance. It can save some squabbling over lights being left on to have the allowance paid to the clergy and let them pay the bills. Use previous years' expenses for establishing this allowance. Every two or three years the minister should present the actual bills to the budget building group to keep the allowance up to date.

## Benefits

### Retirement and Death Benefit Plans

Good stewardship for yourself and your family demands that you participate in a retirement and death benefit plan. Contribute as much as you can as early as you can. In addition to contributions to a retirement account, be sure to provide life insurance for you and your spouse. Individuals who have children at home or in college should be insured for about ten times your annual salary. Term life insurance continues to provide the most coverage for the least investment.

### Medical and Dental Benefits

The current economy is making it increasingly hard for churches to offer health insurance benefits. Please make sure you and your family are covered. If your spouse provides family insurance coverage through his or her employment, ask the church to put a significant part of the money they won't be spending on health insurance into your salary or retirement benefit.

### Social Security and Medicare Tax Offset

This offset is often provided to cover the one-half of the Social Security and Medicare tax that a church cannot pay for ordained persons. Remember, this is taxable income. We suggest that you have the church mail this offset to the Internal Revenue Service using your name and Social Security number. In circumstances where participation in Social Security violates matters of conscience, clergy can opt out. It is Riley's opinion that the disability coverage and death benefit to minors make participation advisable.

## Other Benefits

Insist that the church pay the full IRS-approved reimbursement for auto expenses. This amount can be found each year at www.IRS.gov. Further insist that the church utilize the accountable reimbursement plan; any other pattern will not satisfy the IRS. This requires you to keep written records of miles driven in ministry, and it does not cover miles driven from your home to the ministry or church site. This report is given monthly to the treasurer and the amount is reimbursed tax-free.

A hospitality allowance reimburses ministers for hospitality expenses directly related to their ministry. This includes entertaining church members in your home and some business meals.

If funds are designated for convention or continuing education in the annual statement of income and benefits, that will lower your taxable income. All the allowances and the amount must be in the minutes of congregational business meetings. They must be identified in the business meeting prior to implementation. There is no way to do this retroactively.

Put in writing how many Sundays are included in the vacation granted and have the church state whether or not unused vacation time can be carried over to the next year. Also have the church articulate how many sick days are allowed, at what rate they accumulate, and how many days can be accumulated. The church's view may be that it is hiring a new employee, and ministers view a new position as a transfer within the same company. As a result, churches may offer less vacation than you request. If vacation and sick time become a sticking point in negotiations, remind the search committee that time is the cheapest thing the church can give—and that even (and especially) pastors need Sabbath.

A standard agreement might state that professional employees will receive thirty days of vacation annually and may use only four Sundays annually as vacation. Vacation days must be used in the calendar year they are earned unless otherwise negotiated with the deacons before the end of that year. The vacation schedule will be submitted to church leaders well in advance, and the pastor will leave an accurate phone number when on vacation or out of town.

Additionally, be sure the following items are addressed either in a work agreement or personnel policy. Don't assume, and don't abuse. One pastor Riley worked with had to use vacation time for her surgery and recovery.

Some sample agreements are these:

- The pastor will have two days off each week.
- For sick days, the pastor will begin employment with ten sick days. Sick days will accumulate at a rate of ten days per year of employment and can accumulate up to sixty days. Sick days cannot be used for paid time off.
- The pastor will be granted up to ten days, including one Sunday, for continuing education and will communicate continuing education plans to the deacons.

Over time, all of us will change and our interest in areas of ministry will morph. God opens new doors and grants new gifts. To be faithful to our call we must be open to changes in our ministry priorities. We must be anchored in our call from God to serve, not bound in our call to a specific form of response.

The time to negotiate for a sabbatical leave is at the time you are negotiating with a congregation or agency. If you are fortunate, the church or agency may already have a sabbatical leave process in place. If the church or agency is near or serves a number of educational institutions, people may be comfortable with the conversation, but many are not. If the congregation is unfamiliar with the practice of sabbatical leave, you might put it in the agreement that a sabbatical leave policy will be developed within the first two years. Ask for the help of the judicatory for practices of churches in your region or area. Remember, as you help people consider this, to help the church plan for the sabbatical as well by setting aside dollars that will help with extra expenses during a sabbatical time. Be reasonable in your expectations in terms of length of service before a leave might be granted and number of days away, as well as how much time can be accumulated for such leaves. Marcia knows of one situation where a pastor wanted to be able to go to the mission field every other year to teach for six to ten weeks, so this kind of leave was negotiated at the time of call. Every other year this pastor has gone away with the knowledge and blessing of the church to do a different kind of ministry in a different kind of place. It gives the pastor a different perspective and gives the church a break as well.

When agreements are made, put them into a written document. The clergy and church representatives should sign this document. The search committee is acting on behalf of the church, but make sure your agreements are with the church body, through its leaders. If the search committee does not offer a document, find a workable template and offer it to the search committee for editing. You can find one such sample template at www.judsonpress.com in a downloadable form. This offers a template that can be edited according to your agreement with the church and according to the polity of the church. The websites listed at the end of this chapter also provide examples of work agreements.

The mundane task of determining salary and benefits can sometimes seem to get in the way of discerning God's call. At other times it can seem to override what God says. Be as prayerful in this aspect of considering a call as any other aspect. You need to model that responding to a call in all aspects is a spiritual journey and that it includes negotiation around salary and benefits. You may find that a church or agency may take the lead from you in this process. If you include times of prayer and encouragement during the process, then they may see God at work in the process, too. A negotiation between a candidate and a ministry that can't come to a positive agreement is a "no, don't go there." There are many ways we can receive God's leading.

## Applying the Principles

### *One Mistake at a Time*

In the spring before graduation from seminary, James interviewed and candidated for a church in a nearby state. He was proud of himself because he would be one of the first in his graduating class to have a church when he graduated. He was excited and unsure because this was his first full-time ministry. The church extended a call to him and sent him a work agreement with all of the facts and figures. The salary was modest but workable; however, the church did not include a utilities allowance for the parsonage. James remembered that the committee had told him the church would pay the utilities. He and his wife felt they couldn't manage without the utilities allowance. After discussion, the church would not include money for utilities in the salary package. That proved to be a deal breaker, and James declined the call. He and his wife weren't able to figure out where the process went wrong. Had they remembered incorrectly, or had the church not followed through with the offer made by the search committee? In their next interaction with a potential church they made sure to get all the important information in writing before the candidating weekend.

### Planning Ahead

Karen relocated before Aaron did and rented an apartment. She and Aaron felt they needed to purchase a home to start building equity. They had this feeling before the move, so they had begun saving for their down payment. Living in the community for eight months before Aaron relocated, Karen was able to identify the area of town they would like to live in. She also gained a good understanding of the real estate climate and kept watch for a good deal. When Aaron was called to the new ministry, they knew what they could afford to spend. They made an offer on a house contingent on being called to the church that was considering Aaron. This allowed them to get into the home sooner than waiting until Aaron was called and in town.

### Looking Forward

Sarah and Dom had served churches with parsonages their entire ministry. Sarah was approaching forty-five and realized that in retirement they would not have a home of their own. She felt there were many more years of ministry at her current church, so she didn't want to have to move in order to work toward home ownership.

Sarah took a proposal of an equity agreement to her board at budget time. The church agreed to put $750 each year that Sarah and Dom put a like amount in a two-signature account. This way she could stay at the church, live in the parsonage, and begin to accumulate equity. With the real estate market the way it was, Sarah and Dom were gaining more through the shared savings account than they would if they owned a home in that community. Sarah also realized that every line in the church budget had an advocate except her salary. She began making a recommendation to the finance committee each year. She reasoned that she was in the best position to know what the church could afford and how effective she had been during the previous year. As often as not she got what she suggested.

## Suggestions for Your *Next Steps*

- Are you prepared to have the compensation discussion? If not, what do you need to do to be prepared? Consider setting up a mock interview about compensation in particular.

- What do you need and want from your next ministry experience? What do you need for your continued professional growth? What are your family's needs?

- What are your health insurance needs? How do you expect these to be met by the ministry you are seeking?

- How and when will you articulate these needs to a search committee?

## Suggestions for *Prayer*

- Thank God for the ministries you have had over the years and those who have given generously to support you in those ministries.

- Ask God for guidance as you consider what you need in the years ahead.

• Ask God for wisdom and grace as you seriously consider
need over want. Listen for God's voice as you consider num-
bers and realities of your life.

## Websites

The Ministers Council (American Baptist Churches USA) offers a variety
of helpful resources and document, including the Minister-Church
Agreement found at this link: http://www.ministerscouncil.com/
Brochures/documents/SuggestMinisterChurchAgreementRevised03
.pdf (accessed March 29, 2011).

The Baptist General Convention of Texas provides a complete manual
for pastoral search committees, with supporting sample documents
and forms, including a Minister-Church Covenant. The manual may be
found online at http://texasbaptists.org/education-discipleship/pastorless-
churches/minister-search-committee-reference-guide/ (accessed March
29, 2011).

The Bivocational/Smaller Church Ministry Team website also features a
detailed online manual for pastoral search committees. Included among
its forms (in Appendix 12) is a sample Pastor-Church Covenant. Visit
http://www.bivocational.org/BIVO/index.html and search under the
Pastor Search Menu and tabs (accessed March 29, 2011).

# CHAPTER 9
# Transition Ethics

*Do your best to present yourself to God as one approved by him, a worker who has no need to be ashamed, rightly explaining the word of truth. (2 Timothy 2:15)*

*In this chapter* we will address several items to keep in mind as you participate in the search process for a new call. We begin with stressing that in this day and age people can find out a lot about you just by typing your name in Google Search. Even if you are not currently looking for a new call, you need to keep this in mind in your social networking and online activities.

Riley's mother-in-law had a saying: "You should always tell the truth, but don't always be telling it." Communication is proliferating at a profound rate today, but privacy was an early casualty. When wireless headsets for cell phones were developed, we heard the veil of privacy open. Cell phone users talked loudly into their headsets. They would move around while they talked. Without an invitation, passersby become part of the conversation.

Social networks allow broad and accessible communication. They allow for a wide variety of personal expression. One can think out loud or vent anger and frustration—there is no end to the possibilities. Persons in ministry must be aware that this web presence will preserve any exposed moment in our lives. That moment can and will be accessed by persons who may have interest in us. Our congregants hear us without the filter of context. Potential search committees can get snapshots of our lives and thoughts. We weren't talking to them, but they have the ability to listen. Be very careful. Don't post items you would not say in the presence of your congregants. Posting and talking in public have the same consequence, even if we weren't intending those interested in our ministry to be part of the conversation.

## Denominational Affiliations

Beyond our skills in ministry and the needs we have identified regarding the church or community, there should be a good match if we seek to serve in a denominational context. It is impossible for us to look at a denomination through your priorities and theological lens, so that analysis must be your task. We suggest that you study written material and talk with clergy who have served in that context for a period of time. If you are considering a denomination you have not had experience with, we suggest *The Complete Guide to Christian Denominations: Understanding the History, Beliefs, and Differences* by Ron Rhodes. Please see Appendix C for an overview of various denominational search and call processes.

Most clergy information packets from denominational systems will ask for a response regarding your interest and involvement in the life of the denomination. If you are interested in serving a church in that system and if you are interested in getting your résumé past the gatekeeper, don't check the box that is equivalent to "not important." If you have no interest or intention to support and help to improve a denominational family, serve somewhere else. This is a time in the history of the church when denominations are being deemphasized by our culture. It is a time when denominations are in rapid change. But it appears they still have value to Christ and the church or they would have vanished. Denominations are still here, and God is still using imperfect structures to affect ministry. A denomination will provide ministers a system of support and a family of colleagues. It is of significant service to you and your family when you need to make a transition in ministry. Availability of a single retirement program is important as you transition. There are resources on call and accessible if you reach out. External standards and accountability help us fulfill the high calling of Christ in our ministry.

Another equally egregious violation of clergy ethics occurs when clergy seek to lead a congregation out of their relationship with a denomination. That choice is the purview of the congregation, but not the clergy. Riley asks persons seeking participation in our American Baptist church family, "If you are called to serve in our family and at some point in the future you find that you can no longer serve in good faith, will you resign the church and move on rather than attempting to lead the church out of the family?" When clergy do seek to remove a church from the denominational family, they are elevating their contemporary feeling above a historical and sustained act of God. Riley operates on the assumption that God raised up a church in a particular relationship to other churches. As ministers we can seek service there or somewhere else. But leave the relationships of the church to the body of believers who are there.

Clergy sexual misconduct is probably the most grievous violation of clergy ethics and damages a congregation severely. Ministering in a denominational family significantly increases the likelihood of being caught and held to account. In an independent church, the power accumulated by the clergy can more easily overwhelm a fractured leadership structure. That is not the case where there is organized watch care over the local congregations and those responsible entities are not subject to the influence and authority of offending clergy.

## Integrity

When conversation begins with a church, we recommend that you communicate all significant information early in the process. The issues in your life that might be problematic to a congregation should be presented clearly and early. Secrets can't be kept, but if they could, don't begin a ministry by misrepresenting yourself or your family. If you feel a matter may be a deal breaker for the congregation or for you, it is in your best interest and the best interest of the church to place that issue at the beginning. This will allow the congregation more time to process the information, and it will keep surprises from derailing the process at a later date. It is better for a process to end, if it must, sooner rather than later. If a relationship cannot develop, it is better not to invest energy and anticipation in a situation that can't lead to a call. Your circumstances of leaving congregational ministry will have no bearing on your search for secular employment. It seems best not to inject the information unless asked.

Robert Dingman tells of a role he played while a member of his church's search committee. Dingman left a note in the room of the arriving candidate that called on the candidate to remove himself from the search process if there were anything in that person's life that might do damage to family and ministry if it were found out. He urged the person to use any excuse at hand to withdraw from consideration. The candidate left before the next day's meeting, leaving a note that said there were matters in his life that needed to be disciplined before he could consider a new ministry.[1]

Dingman contends that a number of church leaders have damaged their family and their ministry by serious moral or ethical indiscretions that were later found out. If there are potentially lethal surprises in your life, we urge you to come clean and seek treatment and counseling in order for you to be set free. To have a full life, we must be free from the life trauma and the acting out it causes. If you have not achieved that freedom, please move away from a search process to give priority to treatment and counseling.[2]

## Working with Search Committees

We have seen clergy who failed to respond affirmatively or negatively in a reasonable time to a search committee or congregation. A congregation or an agency can stop the feedback loop, but a ministerial candidate can also stop it. When a candidate stops the process, you leave a group uncertain, and that fact can reflect on all others. If you must say no to a situation, do so. It is unethical to play one church or agency against another. Your sense of call to a situation should be clear. If you need extra time to be sure about the call, negotiate the time you need and be truthful to those who are talking to you so they, too, can discern whether or not they want to continue conversations with you.

Riley has seen clergy stall for time before answering in hopes of receiving a more attractive call. In the most egregious situation, after receiving a call from a church, the minister demanded changes to the church constitution that would give almost unlimited power to the pastoral position. The individual also never responded to the offer of salary and benefits. Eventually the church moderator contacted the candidate and said, "If we don't get an answer from you in a week's time, we will assume you have declined the call and move on." This was very hard for the congregation, because they weren't told that they were being manipulated. As a candidate, be ethical and give a timely answer.

## Communicating the Decision to Transition

The decision to transition in ministry is a private decision lived out in public. When is it best to tell colleagues, friends, and lay persons in the church you are serving? If you have professional colleagues in your current church and supportive and caring relationships, it is a great benefit to you to share with people and seek their feedback. However, if you have strained relationships, you risk being undercut or ousted before it is helpful to you. Communicate your decision to seek another call with other professional staff members in the church you are currently serving. There is a greater intimacy and trust expected of a ministry team that makes this conversation useful and valuable to you. If staff relationships in your current situation are strained, talk with a trusted person about the viability of this communication. Peers and friends should be a part of your considerations. They know you and your ministry; this can be a great blessing to you.

Because the relationship with lay persons in the congregation is different from that of staff, proceed with caution. It is best for clergy to not let it be known to lay persons that they are in the process of moving. If this does become known, two things will likely happen. First, this can be disruptive to the ministry of the church. The congregation will likely quit viewing the future with you in it. It can stall ministry initiatives and follow through on midrange plans. Second, it starts the clock running. Clergy will be expected and possibly pressured to leave in what seems to the church to be a reasonable time. That time frame may or may not be based on reality.

When you have accepted a call, it is time to start notifying people in your current ministry. First inform your key lay person (the chair of deacons, the moderator or chair of the church council). At the first of the week prior to your public resignation, tell your close friends and inform board or committee chairpersons. Ask them to inform the rest of their board before your public resignation. Intentionally letting the information out will help the church prepare for the upcoming resignation. Resignations are hard because it formalizes your leaving a place where you have invested your life and love, and you are leaving people you care for. Work from a written copy of your resignation; don't "just wing it."

Tell persons who have been assisting you and the other churches you have been talking with when you have accepted a call. This demonstration of integrity will be useful to you because you will likely be involved in another search and call process in the same system. Integrity makes an impression.

## Holding a Kingdom View

For persons making their first move, it may feel like you are cheating the church you are serving to use their time to seek out your next ministry. Take a kingdom view rather than an employing church view. Moving from one ministry to another is part of your kingdom service. This may seem a betrayal of close friendships, but it seems best to wait until you have made a final decision to bring members of your current ministry into the conversation. However, also use discretion. If you are thinking that you will be looking at other places, save vacation time to go to interviews and candidating weekends. Don't expect your current church to give you extra time away because you feel led to a new place of service.

It is proper in most systems to talk and interview with several churches at any one time. It is proper to communicate to one church that you are in conversation with other churches. However, once you have accepted a trial sermon or candidating weekend, it is necessary to cease advancing discussions with all other churches. It may be useful for you to view interviewing as dating and accepting an invitation to be the final candidate as an engagement. One can date, with mutual agreement, more than one person at a time, but advancement of other relationships should cease when one of those relationships matures to an engagement. The same rule is true in the search process, provided there is mutual agreement. You should notify all other ministries you are in dialogue with that you have accepted an invitation to be a candidate. And you should notify those that you have contacted during your search process that you have accepted a call and thank them for their assistance even if you were not aware that they did anything. Don't abuse a body of believers by holding open an option while you are waiting for something better to appear. Prayerfully arrive at a yes or no and act on God's leadership. Considering multiple churches and even interviewing can be a useful part of understanding what you seek and do not seek in your next ministry. It is acceptable and even beneficial to use interviews as opportunities to learn and discern—and ultimately decline those ministry positions that you determine are not consistent with God's call.

We learn from the experiences, and so does the search committee. It has happened to many of us that we went to an interview without a compelling sense that "this is the one." Yet, during the interview we became fully aware that God was indeed present and calling us to this ministry.

## Staying in Touch

The search process can be long and frustrating. One thing we can do while we wait is keep in touch with persons who are sharing your résumé with churches. Contacting these key individuals every two months via email or a phone call is appropriate and will keep you on their mind without pestering them. Also let those same individuals know when you have completed your transition.

Be prepared to be patient, be willing to wait for the right one, because your only other choice is foolishness. If we foolishly jump at the best situation we see or the last situation we see on our horizon, we have not trusted God. Searching and seeking God's call is a raw exercise of our faith. Be patient; remember God doesn't wear a wristwatch. Trusting God to lead you through what is on your part a passive process demands faith and maturity. There are ministers who don't appear to have waited on the Lord, and we know of ministries that therefore have lasted only six weeks.

## Leaving Your Current Ministry

Tell the ministry you are leaving that you will not be available to do ministry without the invitation of your successor. This creates necessary space for our successor to bond with the congregation. Healthy clergy ethics allow us to remain friends with former congregants but not to remain in a pastoral or advisory role. It is meddling when we continue to exert influence in a church we have left. Understanding that God has led you away from the former congregation mandates the cessation of input to that congregation. If you keep coming back, you will compromise the process of your successor filling the role he or she was called to.

What we are asked to do will vary according to our previous role and gifts. It is reasonable to say yes to an invitation to do a wedding or a funeral or to provide music for close friends. Even in the cases of close friendship, however, it is best to involve your successor in the event. Please remember, we have a few friends, and most are congregants that we cared for. It is reasonable to continue these strong relationships, but we must guard against offering counsel regarding the congregation and its ministry. If you want to continue your pastoral involvement in the life of the congregation, don't resign. You can't have it both ways. See the next chapter for further suggestions on how to articulate the separation agreement.

Seek an opportunity for an exit interview. At the point of your resignation you are arguably the most informed person about doing ministry in your particular setting. The institution can benefit from your feedback regarding working relationships and the effectiveness of the established ministries. It will be best to discuss items that you can be objective about. Ask your governing board for the chance to sit down with a couple of influential members for this conversation. The second best option is to have the conversation with a denominational person who can give the information to the church at a proper time.

A useful exit interview would include answering the following questions:

1. What was most satisfying about your job?
2. What was least satisfying about your job?
3. Did your job description accurately reflect your responsibilities? If not, what responsibilities should have been added (or omitted)?
4. Did you receive adequate support to do your job? If not, what additional support would have been helpful?
5. Did you receive sufficient feedback about your performance? If not, what additional feedback would have been helpful?
6. What would you change to make our work life better?
7. Were you happy with your pay, benefits, and other incentives? Why or why not?
8. What church policies or procedures or practices made your job more difficult?
9. Did anyone discriminate against you, harass you, or cause hostile working conditions? If so, are you willing to provide more information?

The transition time and all of its interactions are under the sovereignty of God. There is no reason for us to manipulate or skew a process. If we trust God, then trust God to work through a process to lead you.

A search and call process is very much under the sovereignty of God. Thus we as servants of God must bring our entire high calling to this process. Doing ministry is an exercise of trusting God, trusting God's people, and trusting God's institutions. As worthy servants of God, we need to hold to the values God expects of us and not try shortcuts driven by expediency or need.

## Applying the Principles

### Stay Out of the Way

Brennan was called to serve on a judicatory staff. At the time he accepted this call, his children were nearing the end of high school. He got permission from his supervisor to work from his home and not move until after their graduation. He was careful not to maintain the same social and recreational relationships he had when he was serving the church in that town. There were only two very close relationships that he maintained. His presence in town was no hindrance to either the interim minister or the calling of the next pastor. He stayed out of the way.

### Exit Interview

Grace has been asked to schedule an exit interview in the weeks following her resignation. She knows this interview is important, but she is concerned about two things. Her relationship with a fellow staff member has caused her a great deal of pain, and she wants to give her best insight to the church leaders. Grace is going to ask the committee for the questions so she can offer considered responses in writing. She wants to meet their expectations, so she will ask for a face-to-face meeting, where she will submit her written responses and clarify anything the exit committee wants.

### Balanced Priorities

James was serving his third church when he was diagnosed with a chronic but manageable illness. He and his wife, Anna, went to a nearby research hospital, where they developed good relationships with the doctors and staff. Additionally, he was able to receive cutting-edge treatment. The church was supportive of James and the lifestyle adjustments he had to make. James and Anna began to realize that if they left this church, they would limit their search to stay within sixty miles of the hospital.

### Who Are You Serving?

Len was ready to move. He had served a church for five years following a fifteen-year ministry at one of the largest congregations in his state. That ministry had given him national exposure, which he enjoyed. A substantial church was wooing him to be its pastor. He indicated he was very much interested but needed more time to make up his mind. He used the next sixty days to wait for a denominational search committee to invite him to serve in a prominent judicatory position. It appeared that he was keeping the church waiting so he could look further. When his unethical behavior came to light, he lost all credibility among his denominational colleagues, and the new church withdrew their call.

### God Is Doing a New Thing

Tonya completed seminary and was contacted by a church from another denomination. She declined the call and recommended a friend to the committee. She wasn't familiar with the new denomination and had never considered serving in a context other than her denomination of origin. Contacted by the church again, Tonya again declined. She was having an internal struggle because she felt attracted to the church but her spouse was highly resistant to serving in a new denomination. Eventually she resolved her inner struggle. She told her husband, Sam, she had come to the realization that she either had to serve the denomination that educated her or the God who called her. That understanding allowed her to contact the church in good faith and ask it to put her résumé on the bottom of its stack of names. If the committee members worked through the other names and came to her, she was willing to be considered. Tonya and Sam made the move into a new church and a new denomination.

## Suggestions for Your *Next Steps*

- Are you prepared to be forthright with a search committee? Why or why not?

- Consider having a conversation with a trusted friend, counselor, or colleague before you begin the journey to new relationships.

## Suggestions for *Prayer*

- Thank God for the ministry and the people you have ministered to thus far in your life. Remember especially those who taught you important lessons in ministry.

- Ask God to give you wisdom and grace as you journey on the process of a new call.

- Ask God to help you to remember always those with whom you are doing ministry and to prepare you for your new ministry.

### NOTES

1. Robert W. Dingman, *The Complete Search Committee Guidebook* (Ventura, CA: Regal Books, 1989), 161–62, used by permission.

2. Ibid., 154.

# CHAPTER 10
# Resignation and the Time Between

Create in me a clean heart, O God, and put a new and right spirit within me. (Psalm 51:10)

*We've spent most* of the book looking at the discernment and search processes. This chapter assumes that you have been called to a new situation. This can seem like a new journey, even though you may have been working toward this the whole time! Leaving well is as important as entering a ministry well. There is a saying that the last impression is the one that lasts. It is important, no matter what the relationship you had in your present position, to say goodbye and to be aware that the congregation or agency is one that continues even if you are not there.

When the decision is made to resign, how you do it and what you put in a resignation letter can make a big difference about how your ministry is perceived whether or not the resignation is because of good reasons (moving to another situation, a sense of call to another place) or a forced resignation. A resignation letter ought to acknowledge the good things learned in the situation. It should express thanksgiving for the time spent within the faith community. Resignation letters that take potshots or lay blame ultimately reflect negatively on the person who wrote the letter.

One of the best resignations Marcia ever witnessed was in the midst of intense conflict in a church between some leaders and the pastor. Despite the tension, however, the pastor announced his resignation at the Sunday morning worship service. He indicated when he would be leaving. He thanked the people for the time he had with them and acknowledged that although there had been a fair amount of pain, he truly cared for the congregation, their work, and their mission. He told them he did not know what he would do next, but he did not dwell there. Instead, he focused on the good that he had gained. He also asked four people who were present in worship and had given him a good amount of pain to come forward. He made a public apology to all of them. He asked for their forgiveness and asked that the hatchets be buried at least for a month so the church and he could say the goodbyes they needed to say. Although this action did not put an end to the pain, it helped prepare everyone involved for the healing process.

Even if your resignation is going to happen, we recommend that you don't announce your resignation until you have a signed separation agreement in place with the leaders of your church or agency. You lose all leverage for negotiation after you resign. Severance that includes salary for a specified time and continuation of health insurance is certainly in your best interests, and in a church context, such a package may also comfort those members who support you, knowing that the congregation is making some provision for you and your family in the transition. If you live in church-owned housing, be sure to negotiate how long you can remain and who is responsible for utilities. When you make a deal, adhere to its terms.

Resign at the time required by your work agreement. When a resignation is given, forward progress in the ministry with you as leader significantly diminishes, for people begin the separation process.

## Don't Offer or Threaten to Resign

If you offer to resign, you might well be taken up on the offer. Once you resign, in the minds of many people the clock starts running, measuring time until you leave. Threatening to resign is like a child threatening to hold his or her breath. As a child, Riley used to play dominos with his grandfather. Sometime he would put out a domino and then try to take it back. His grandfather would say, "A domino laid is a domino played." It's the same way with resignation.

When you have a choice, don't resign until you have a place to go. It is always easier to get a call when you are active in ministry. Raising this issue will break the trust inherent in your call. It is also unwise to offer to resign until you are prepared to facilitate an orderly transition. If leaving your current ministry and seeking other position *is* in the best interests of your family or of the congregation or organization you serve, please remember that the search and call process requires time. In the vast majority of situations you, your family, and the ministry will be better off if the transition can be done decently and in order.

The purpose of not telling anyone at all before you are ready to announce your resignation is to honor your confidential relationships, to avoid an unnecessary shock to the congregation, and to build your separation agreement. Once you tell someone, the word will get out, and it puts people in difficult situations. When you know that you need to develop the separation agreement, begin with one key leader. Then, in the week preceding your public resignation, you may confide in close friends among church members or professional colleagues.

## Don't React from Feeling Alone

A reaction based in anger, hurt, or outrage is unlikely to serve anyone well, especially you. It will inevitably create a deeper wound—in your spirit and in the life of the congregation or organization. Think before you respond. At least tell people you will get back to them with your response. This will give you time to seek counsel from peers and contact your support persons.

All too often, ministers will act hastily, trying to avoid conflict or to solve the problem alone. Especially in a church context, contact a third-party support or intervention entity, denominational resources, a respected pastor, or a respected community leader. Their involvement will facilitate discernment about the issues, the extent of congregational support for the minister's departure, and arrangements for structuring the transition in terms of time frame and a separation agreement. At the very least, involvement of this third party will buy some time for you to plan your transition.

## Don't Allow Yourself to Be Bullied

Again, knowing your rights per the guiding documents of the church or organization will give you solid ground to stand on. Learn what your options are and what authority different individuals or groups in the church or organization hold.

If your situation is building in negativity, it may be necessary to tell the leaders of your current congregation or organization that you are in the process of seeking another place to serve. This should be done only to buy you more time to seek another call. Informing the church you are leaving often will temporally lessen the pressure. It will buy limited time, and it may be helpful to suggest that the process can take six to nine months. It is best if a third party can play the role of a broker. This action can be taken only once with a congregation, so do not choose to use it unless you are serious about finding a new call.

## Let Your Resignation Be a Resignation

Offer your formal resignation at a time when the largest portion of the congregation is together. This will allow as many people as possible to hear the resignation from you. It is also reasonable to give a written copy of your resignation to the church. We even recommend that you put a formal written message in the mail so that it will get into mailboxes the day after the formal announcement. You can also send an email after the verbal announcement. The purpose of a formal notice of resignation is to notify the congregation or organization of the upcoming end of your ministry among them, to fulfill the conditions of your work agreement (written or unwritten), and to express thanks for the time you had with the congregation. We recommend wording such as this for your formal resignation:

It has been my privilege to serve my Lord and this congregation [or organization] for the past ___ years. I would like to publicly inform the congregation [or my colleagues] that I have accepted a position as _____ at _____ and that my last day of ministry here will be _____. I have appreciated my time serving God with you. May God continue to guide and bless us both. Thank you.

If this is an involuntary termination or if you are resigning but do not have future employment arranged, use a similar statement indicating that you are seeking God's guidance for your next place of ministry.

When you tell the church you are leaving, tell them that once you leave you will not be available to do funerals or weddings without the invitation of your successor. Healthy clergy ethics allow us to remain friends with former congregants but not to remain in a pastoral or advisory role. Understanding that God has led you away from the former congregation mandates the cessation of input to that congregation.

In all cases, this will be an emotional moment, so be prepared. This public statement is intended as a simple notification of those who will be most directly affected by your transition—church members or those who are the primary receivers of your ministry. Some members may be shocked; some may plead with you to reconsider for their sakes. Be ready to continue to offer pastoral care, knowing that you may have your own emotions to work through at the same time. Be open with your emotions of care and concern and sadness of leaving. By contrast, members of the congregation who haven't heard you before won't hear you now. If you indulge your anger, hurt, or disappointment in a public way, in all likelihood the good folks and the ministry of the church will be hurt. Scripture tells us, "Simply let your 'Yes' be 'Yes,' and your 'No,' 'No'; anything beyond this comes from the evil one" (Matthew 5:37, NIV). That advice applies readily to ministry transitions. Let your resignation be a resignation.

It is more likely than any minister wants to admit that, at some point during our life's ministry, we will be asked to resign. Please remember that such a request may or may not come to fruition. When asked by an individual or by a small group, take some time to assess the critique and the critics. It is relatively rare that even a vocal minority can unilaterally dismiss a minister called by the congregation. However, if you have lost the support of significant leaders, your ministry in that place is almost certainly done. You may win the next battle, but you have lost the war. Conserve all the time you can for use in the placement process.

When a request for your resignation comes from a supervisor, an official board, or a congregational vote, check the guiding documents of the organization—the church constitution, by-laws, or employee manual. Know who has the authority to terminate your service and the process by which such termination must be effected. Even when a forced transition seems inevitable, keep in mind the three don'ts: Don't threaten or offer to resign; don't react from feeling alone; and don't allow yourself to be bullied.

## Request an Exit Interview

As discussed in the previous chapter, *do* seek an opportunity for an exit interview with a member of your staff relations committee or other leaders of the church or agency you serve. Make the most of your exit interview. Don't use it to air your personal grievances. Be constructive in your leave-taking. At the point of your resignation you are arguably the most informed persons about doing ministry in your particular setting. The institution can benefit from your feedback regarding working relationships and effectiveness of the established ministries. It will be best to discuss items that you can be objective about. Ask your governing board for the chance to sit down with a couple of influential members for this conversation. The second best option is to have the conversation with a denominational person who can give the information to the church at a proper time.

## The Time Between

A critical time is the interval between the announcement of your resignation and the date that you leave your current ministry. During this time, you must remain faithful to the current ministry and to God who called you to that place of service. A useful principle to guide ministers in a transition is to do your job without working into the future.

This time between will require some reallocations of energy and priority. While you are still in your current position, it is necessary to keep doing necessary ministries. As long as you remain in the ministry, you are accepting the responsibility to minister faithfully to the needs of the people. Keep pointing the way, but don't push. Shift your priorities to pastoral care in the congregation and taking care of yourself. Pastoral care must continue until the day you depart, but the time between is not a season for visionary planning, pushing an agenda, or lobbying for change or resolution of conflict.

Backing away gently likely will cause active resistance from leaders and the congregation to minimize. From a kingdom perspective, this time between is a necessary time for recharging your energies. You will encounter the emotional and physical challenges of packing and moving geographically. It is important to acknowledge and address the grief associated with leave-taking and the mixed emotions around reasons for the transition.

The church will be dealing with its grief, and you can find opportunities to rest and allow yourself to coast for a time. We must have energy and resources to invest in our new situation. In this time between, don't rehearse what isn't working in the ministry you are leaving. It is useful to begin looking beyond where you are toward the possibilities you may be called to. Take care to work toward healing the hurts that you have accumulated. Forgive yourself, and try to forgive those who have hurt you. Don't take hurts with you; they will just burden your future ministry. Leave behind that which will not serve you in a new place.

Use this "time between" for productive introspection; refocus on what you are called to do and what you are not. It is essential that we have this inner guidance so we won't wind up in a situation that doesn't fit or a ministry pattern that uses us up. Please keep in mind that a preference or comfort zone for you is not a kingdom mandate.

A transition in ministry has some parallels with transitions in business or industry. In both situations, you will announce your resignation in advance of your departure, and in many instances, you are expected to facilitate the transition through an information transfer. In business and industry, that transfer may be in writing or in person, through training your successor. In the church, it is far more common that the information will be transferred to a select individual or group of lay leaders who will handle pastoral care in the interim. While any transition demands integrity, ministry transitions require special measures of integrity with regard to relationships. Take time to honor and celebrate the context God has called you to serve. The question, "How do I remain and feel faithful to my call while I am disengaging, searching, and re-engaging in another ministry?" is particularly conflicting for clergy who haven't moved before. The best advice we have to give is to pay attention to where you are, rather than to anticipate the possibilities of where you are going. Paying attention is particularly true of relationships more than the mundane working of the church or ministry.

The disengaging that occurs prior to leaving a particular ministry is a consolidation phase of ministry. During this time it is useful to focus on empowering lay leaders and ministries. Give them both affirmation and space. It is a time of continuation of the core ministries of pastoral care and worship, but it is not a time to initiate new issues. If lay leaders raise ministry advancements or maturations, encourage them and empower them to take their own necessary steps.

Disengagement is also done because you will need both emotional and physical energy to engage a new ministry. Slowing down your pace in this time between won't harm the ministry you are leaving and may help you to serve the ministry you are being called to.

Disengagement is done with the understanding that the search process and inherent with discernment take both emotional and physical energy. It is reasonable to claim the needed emotional resources for the process. This is a time for reflection of your ministry. Where were you strong? Where have you grown? What area do you know you need to grow in?

Prepare to pay the price of caring. Because you learned to care for the people in your current ministry, it is hard to intentionally end many of those relationships. This is an ongoing cost of ministry; relationships are formed, valued, and then ended. It might seem wiser not to invest in the people you minister with. But from God's perspective, why would you be called to serve a new group if you had not demonstrated love for and valuing of the previous group? This is one of the hard places of life for clergy. Be willing to honor and process the grief you are experiencing.

## Grief and Loss

As clergy, most of us can recite from memory the stages of grief,[1] but can we apply these stages to our experience of transitioning from a specific ministry? Grief is our emotional response to the loss of anything important to us. It is important for us to be in touch with our grief. Our experience of grief will begin when we agree with God that it is time to transition. This will put you and your family at a very different place from that of the congregation you serve. You have begun the grief process, but the people in your ministry setting have not.

If you are forced to leave a specific ministry, it is possible that your anger will be intense. Remember that anger is part our grief and not just a matter of being angry with individuals. The trauma of being forced to leave may intensify your anger. Make sure you aren't spraying this anger on everything surrounding you. It is perfectly fine to focus your anger on those who did indeed hurt you. This is a healthy expression of anger.

Leaving congregational ministry can trigger a deep response. We are leaving or losing what has been our life plan before and all through our training. It is recommended that you seek counseling support to address your grief. If you find yourself stuck at one stage of grief or are moving forward and regularly cycling back to a previous stage of the grief process, it is necessary for you to get counseling support.

## The First Days in a New Church

The first days in a new church can be empowering and confusing. You are wise to set the pace, rather than letting others set the pace. If you can, develop a list of those you want to speak to in your first days of ministry. Develop a process of getting to know the people of the congregation or agency that you will be serving. Figure out early on who can best help you with these tasks. The call and arrival of a new minister is a time of great expectation and hope. One of the things that you are likely to experience is a family or group that exhibits hyperhospitality. These persons possibly bring unrealistic expectations to the developing relationship. They may be part of a church segment that seeks inordinate influence over the ministry. When their expectations are not met to their satisfaction, they will often turn on you. Because their needs were not met to their expectation, they can often be mean and hurtful.

Remember from day one that you were called there to serve the whole congregation, not a segment. We can be easily seduced if the special treatment of that segment satisfies or strokes our ego. That is why it is best to go in with a plan to build relationships with the whole of the congregation or agency. Find a way to work your plan, and remember that the early days are days of listening more than telling them your plans. Even if they ask for your plans, solicit from them what they are expecting; then you might be able to better invite them into your sense of what God is calling you both to do.

Be prayerful in the first days of your new ministry, upholding the new people you meet but also and especially yourself and your family as you seek your way in this new ministry place. Enjoy your new place.

## Last Words

In these pages, we have attempted to help the minister in transition. We know we haven't covered every scenario or possible situation. We hope that the reader will take seriously our counsel to consult God in every way possible and to consult trusted friends, family, and colleagues on the way. This is not a time to go it alone; do your work with a wealth of consultations with the right persons. Transitions are a time to build connections and listen in ways that might be new to you.

We know that there are many times in the process where you have to sit and wait for God's time or a church's time or an agency's time. It may not be according to your time. Marcia felt that Evergreen Association, where she currently serves, took much too long to make their decision to call her, but that was something that she had to hold close, share with friends who weren't part of the organization, and use the time as an opportunity to grow in grace (i.e., work on her spiritual life, getting closer to God, relying on God's presence and assurance that all would be well). Even though Marcia believes God wants the best for each of God's children, she knows that this is often hard to remember during the search and call process, especially for ministers who are searching. Our best advice is to find that friend or mentor who can hold your hand and heart during the transition time. Find that person who can be pastor and friend to you. Pray to find such a person before you need to search so the person may be there for you during the process.

Resignation is an event that requires all of the personal and spiritual maturity God has granted us. Riley saw a billboard that reminds us, "Remember, God bats last." It is not worthy of our calling as servants of God to vent our hurts or lash out at those who have hurt us. God knows, enough said.

The last good word is to trust God in the process. Transition can be a time of knowing God in ways that you may not have known before. God is faithful. May you know God's blessing and hope as you seek to serve God wherever you are.

## Applying the Principles

### A Time for Everything

Bruce was in a good situation, but he felt it was time to move on—at least some of the time. He candidated for a church and was extended a strong call to be an associate. The next Sunday, he announced his resignation to accept another position. The following Sunday, he told the church he had just resigned from that he had made a mistake and wanted to stay there. They wanted him to stay, so things were all right for a while. As professional church leaders we need to accept the responsibility for knowing when we need to make a transition in ministry. When we are feeling ambivalent, it is best if we not circulate our résumé. Leaving our résumé in circulation but turning down all contacts will cause judicatories not to present us to new situations.

## Suggestions for Your *Next Steps*

- The decision is made. Make a list of who needs to be told, decide the order, and decide how they should be told and when.

- You might also make a list and carry through on giving thanks to those who helped you through the process.

- Did we mention, "make lists"? In the time of transition it is easy to lose some thoughts.
  —What do I need to do in the situation I am leaving?
  —What do I need to prepare for the ministry I am going to?
  —What do I need to remember regarding moving?
  —What do I need to do to make the move easy for my family?

## Suggestions for *Prayer*

- Thank God for the process you have been through and God's faithfulness through the process.

- Thank God for all those who assisted you in the process.

- Ask God for continuing grace and insight as you make the transition from one place to the next, particularly giving you words of comfort for those you are leaving and words of wisdom in the first days in a new position.

NOTE

1. **Shock:** initial paralysis at hearing bad news; **denial:** trying to avoid the inevitable; anger: frustrated outpouring of bottled-up emotion; **bargaining:** seeking in vain for a way out; **depression:** final realization of the inevitable; **acceptance:** finally finding the way forward; **hope:** I will find good in my future.

# Giftedness in Ministry

Take time to identify your understanding of how God has gifted you for ministry. Identify the top eight areas of giftedness in order.

_____ Prepare and implement budget. (budget/financial management)

_____ Develop and maintain programs and activities for enlarging the membership and/or the vision and ministry for the church. (church growth)

_____ Gather together a new body of believers on a regular basis for Bible study and worship which will lead to a new permanent congregation. (church planting)

_____ Keep persons informed through the use of the media, newsletters, etc. (communication)

_____ Identify and evaluate the needs of the community and work to meet those needs through individual and/or corporate action. (community assessment/involvement)

_____ Resolve conflict situations with persons and groups for the sake of the church's ministry. (conflict management)

_____ Provide opportunities (a place and/or persons) for an individual, couples, families, and/or groups to enter a healing relationship. (counseling)

_____ Work with a language, ethnic, or cultural group different from your own. (cross cultural involvement/mission)

_____ Provide a teaching ministry that is based on theological, educational, and historical foundations. (education)

_____ Seek to lead persons to make decisions for Christ, encouraging their identification with and participation in the local church/community. (evangelism)

_____ Cooperate with churches/leaders from Baptist and other denominations. (interchurch cooperation)

_____ Communicate a comprehensive understanding of the Bible and Christian theology in terms relevant to persons' lives. (interpreting the faith)

_____ Seek to recognize and call forth the potential of persons as leaders, providing opportunities for their training and growth. (leadership development)

_____ Attempt to turn vision into reality and to sustain it in the church. (leadership)

_____ Motivate and support persons in discovering and using their gifts for ministry in their daily lives. (ministry of the laity development)

_____ Encourage and provide opportunities for the congregation/individual to be informed and involved in Christian witness at home and abroad. (mission promotion)

_____ Have and demonstrate keen sensibilities to other language, ethnic, and/or cultural groups and settings. (multicultural sensitivity)

_____ Maintain a choral and/or instrumental program/s of the church. (music directing/performing)

_____ Create an atmosphere in which persons feel accepted, included, cared for, and can identify with the group. (nurturing fellowship)

_____ Develop and implement the goals and objectives of the church. (planning and management)

_____ Provide by word and presence an empathetic understanding of and concern for persons in the routine and joys as well as the crises and transitions of life, giving assistance where appropriate and feasible. (pastoral care)

_____ Enable the staff to accomplish their duties and responsibilities and encourage their personal and professional growth. (personnel supervision)

_____ Support the preaching ministry with time for preparation/reflection on the Word, and commitment to listen for the Word's power and its implications for individuals, the church, the community, and the world. (preaching)

_____ Design, encourage, and help to implement organizational, social, educational, religious, and/or recreational programs of ministry. (program development)

_____ Seek to be aware of justice issues in the community and the world, then discover ways to act toward eliminating the causes of injustice. (social action enablement)

_____ Provide opportunities for individuals or groups to understand and enhance the spiritual dimensions of their personal lives. (spiritual life development)

_____ Enable persons to develop and use individual and corporate resources: personal gifts, skills, and finances to the glory of God. (stewardship)

_____ Enable persons to lead using methods and materials appropriate for the learner's age and situation. (teaching)

_____ Make formal and informal connections with church members or others in their homes, at work, or in other settings. (visitation)

_____ Participate actively in worship, offering feedback and suggestions for greater participation and effectiveness in the expression of praise, thanksgiving, and devotion to God. (worship preparation and leading)

_____ Develop and lead a ministry with adolescents which nurtures youth toward Christian faith. (youth ministry).[1]

NOTE

1. Mary Mild, ed., *Calling an American Baptist Pastor* (Valley Forge, PA: National Ministries, 2004), 63–64. Used by permission of ABPS.

# Sample Job Description

## Job Description: Minister or Senior Minister

**Introduction:** The minister or senior minister gives direction and supervision to the total program of the church and to this end should keep in close touch with all other staff members and with all organizations and leaders of the church.

The senior minister is pastor, preacher, challenger, trainer, teacher, enabler, initiator, and guide. However, he or she works with many other members of the body who also minister to one another and the world.

Since each church and each minister is unique, every church's position description would show variance in some areas of leadership and expectations. The educational qualifications for those who are professional church leaders include a college degree and a master of divinity degree or its equivalent. Salaries and benefits, such as retirement, health insurance, professional expenses such as conference expense, continuing education, and time off, will vary in churches of varying size and ability to pay. Such items should be negotiated and agreed upon with the minister at the time of employment, and reviewed at least annually.

Responsibilities, accountabilities, and opportunities for service need to be clarified with position descriptions for all professional staff persons, as well as with expectations and responsibilities of laity and their mutual responsibilities.

## Theology of Ministry

The theme of ministering is found throughout the Scriptures. There are functional differences between apostles, prophets, teachers, and pastors and the general body of disciples, but the concept of the one body was and is the important image of the church. There is the call of God to the individual to be set apart as God's servant in ministry, and there is the validating corporate call of a specific church to the individual to serve in a designated position as a minister to and with a congregation. Such ministry is founded in the ministry that Jesus provided: prophet, priest, and wise ruler. Therefore, ministers are preachers, teachers, leaders, and servants for our Lord Jesus Christ.

### The Senior Minister is:

Accountable to the church, corporately, who calls him or her, and possibly with special accountability to the board or committee that determines the policy and personnel for the local congregation, such as the board of deacons, official board, or staff relations committee.

Accountable with fellow staff members as a team and the congregation as a family for the total ministry of the local church life and the mission to the community and world.

Accountable with the denomination, city, state, regional, and national leaders and ecumenical groups, for meaningful participation in programs and events and the support of same.

Accountable with the pastoral or staff relations committee for cooperative and effective ministries and relationships.

Accountable for:

*Worship Services*
1. Preaching
2. Worship leadership
3. Administration of ordinances
4. Officiating at weddings and funerals

*Teaching Role*
1. Teaching (Bible study, membership classes)
2. Training leaders
3. Evangelistic, ethical, or discipleship concerns and issues
4. Premarital counseling

*Pastoral Care*
1. Visitation (evangelism, homes, hospital(s), nursing homes)
2. Ministry to the bereaved

*Administration*
The minister is responsible for administration of the total church program, though many of the duties of administration will be delegated to staff or volunteer leaders. The minister shall:

1. Assist officers, boards, and committees with long-range and short-term planning and execution of their tasks by consulting, advising, coordinating, and evaluating.
2. Provide for office administration through staff or volunteers for assignments such as central record keeping of minutes, membership records, etc. for all boards, committees, and church business meetings as well as reports of church officers.
3. Function as leader of the staff in cases where there are part-time or full-time paid staff and will be held accountable for building effective staff relationships and for delegating ministries performed by staff. All are colleagues in ministry, and the senior minister is only the first among equals, not above the others. The senior minister should enable each staff member to utilize his or her gifts in the ministry of the church.

*Denominational and Interdenominational Activities*
1. Participate in and cooperate with clusters or associations, city, state, regional, and national programs, events, and activities.
2. Cooperate with other local churches in appropriate ecumenical efforts and witness. Be involved in other community agencies and programs.
3. Support denominational programming and institutions.

*Personal Growth and Recreation*

1. Appropriate time for personal reading, research, and meditation.
2. Plan for and complete two continuing education units (CEU) or the equivalent annually.
3. Use all vacation time allocated by church each year.
4. Have one to two days off each week.
5. Attend denominational and interdenominational conferences and conventions regularly and encourage other staff persons and members of the congregation to do likewise.

## Evaluation

There will be periodic review (annually) with staff persons and staff relations committee. Such appraisal on the part of the minister as well as the church leader group can increase effectiveness as well as improve communications. Job descriptions are likely to be rewritten when there are changes in staff. Evaluation can be a positive and growing experience with emphasis on the positive qualities of leadership, the achieving of objectives, and the determining of new objectives. Un-reached objectives or weaknesses in leadership can be discussed, in love and with plans for improvement.[1]

NOTE

1. http://www.ministerscouncil.com/ClergyCongregationResources/MinisterorSeniorMinister.aspx (accessed September 22, 2010).

# Denominational Processes for Search and Call

## Baptist Conventions

Among Baptists, all local congregations are autonomous. While there are core common beliefs, the variety in congregations gives rise to multiple local church patterns and practices in their search and call process. Here we offer basic overviews of the search and call process for the largest Baptist Conventions.

**American Baptist Churches USA (ABCUSA)** offers direct assistance to local churches in the search and call process. The ABCUSA uses a common résumé from American Baptist Personnel Service (ABPS).[1] The process is based on gifts and skills. Churches are asked to discern what gifts and skills they feel led by God to seek in their next minister. The clergy are asked how they feel God has gifted them for ministry. The regions provide the résumés of persons who are good matches. The local search committee is then responsible for discerning the right person that God is leading them to call. The committee is encouraged to interview multiple persons at the same time but limit their focus to one person to present to the congregation. The congregational vote is the actual call. ABCUSA affirms women in ministry, but congregational acceptance has been sluggish.

**The Baptist General Conference (BGC): Converge Worldwide** encourages congregations and pastors alike to begin their search and call process by contacting their region.[2] The district executive minister is engaged in the process by invitation. A pastoral search committee is formed and organized. The pastoral search committee leads the church to reflect and articulate where it is now and where it wants to go as a church. The committee also identifies the pastoral qualities it will be seeking.

Churches receive ministerial profiles through the district executive. The search committee then prioritizes the candidates and has telephone interviews with the strongest candidates. From the strongest interviewees, the search committee goes to the candidate's church for worship, or they may choose to view a video of worship. If a final candidate is identified, that pastor and spouse are invited for a candidating weekend. A congregational vote usually occurs three to seven days later. Female clergy serve in many roles; however, it is uncommon for BGC churches to consider or call women as pastors.

**Cooperative Baptist Fellowship (CBF)** offers assistance in the search and call process through a broad matching process. The criteria used are Sunday school size and church budget and salary. CBF Reference and Referral is the resource offered to churches. Leader Connect-CBF is the résumé matching service offered by Cooperative Baptist Fellowship.[3] Local search committees then check references, interview, and recommend candidates to their church for consideration of a call. Affirmation of women in ministry was one of the founding principles of the CBF.[4]

**Southern Baptist Convention (SBC)** congregations are receiving increasing support from associations and state conventions in their search and call process. However, the primary vehicle is networking with other churches and key pastors. Clergy submit their résumé directly or through colleagues to the church where a vacancy exists. Search and call functions from the experience and skills of committee members.

Southern Baptists generally affirm that women's role is not identical to that of men in every respect and that pastoral leadership is assigned to men. Clergy who are women serve in most other positions within SBC life.[5]

**National Baptist Convention, USA, Inc. (NBCUSA),** the largest of the historically black Baptist conventions and second only to the Southern Baptist Convention among Baptist groups, offers a web-based ministry and employment opportunities listing.[6] The stated

intention is "bringing together the right person for the right opportunities." That webpage includes a disclaimer that clarifies: "The
National Baptist Convention, USA, Inc. publishes résumés and open
ministry and employment opportunities as a service to its con-
stituent members who are seeking ministry opportunities/employ-
ment or individuals to fill open positions. The Convention does not
pre-qualify potential employers or individuals seeking positions,
nor can it attest to the accuracy of the information presented." In
other words, the website is a listing only, and the convention
"reserves the right to refuse publication of any ministry opportunity
or résumé at its sole discretion."

While the Convention has no published statement concerning
women in ordained ministry, anecdotal evidence suggests that leadership has traditionally been reserved for men, but there is freedom
in the local congregation to ordain and call women to pastoral
ministry.

**Progressive National Baptist Convention (PNBC)** is the second
largest historically black Baptist group. The PNBC facilitates the
search and call process for ministers and congregations through
their regional organizations, although the denominational website
also features a listing of congregational vacancies.7 (For those congregations and clergy that are dually aligned with the ABCUSA, the
American Baptist Personnel Services are available as an additional
resource.) The PNBC does ordain women to pastoral ministry,
although its national and regional leadership at present appears to
be predominantly (if not exclusively) male. If you are a minister
seeking a call within this convention, it is recommended that you
contact the region where you are affiliated for assistance and entry
into the process.

## Other Congregational Denominations and Traditions

**Assemblies of God** congregations each have the right of self-gover-
nance. Thus each congregation calls its pastor. Ministers from other
groups may apply to credentials committee of the General Council
and District Council. These councils are under no obligation to

accept an applicant's previous ministerial status. It is required that applicants be residents of districts where they make application. It is also required that ministers who receive Assembly of God recognition relinquish with any other organization. Local church ministers play a very important role in the process of recognizing and affirming those from outside the Assemblies family. The entry point would be relationships with Assembly of God pastors and the district superintendent. In the life of Assemblies of God, women are eligible for whatever grade of credentials their qualifications warrant. They have the right to administer the ordinances of the church and eligible to serve in all levels of ministry.[8]

**Church of the Brethren** congregations depend on districts to provide assistance in calling pastors. The district also assists congregations in establishing and maintaining healthy pastor-congregation relationships and in mediating problems that develop in those relationships. The district executive/minister provides counseling and assistance to pastors and congregations who enter into contractual and covenantal agreements with each other.

Ministers who desire to engage in ministry in the Church of the Brethren and want to enter the placement process are interviewed by the Ministry Inquiry Committee and the District Ministry Commission and approved by the district board before the candidate's profile is entered into the system.[9]

Church of the Brethren encourages and challenges congregations and districts to treat men and women equally when they search for and call ordained leaders to fill pastoral vacancies.[10]

**Christian and Missionary Alliance (C&MA)** qualifications for pastoral ministry include a specific call to serve God, evidence of a godly lifestyle, and an understanding of and commitment to the mission vision and distinctives of C&MA. Clergy are expected to abstain from use of alcohol and tobacco and any addictive practices.[11] Applicants wishing to transfer from another denomination need to apply through the local district superintendent. Applicants will demonstrate commitment to the mission, vision, and distinctives of the C&MA, as well as submission to constituted authority as defined by C&MA.[12] Throughout the history of the C&MA,

various types of ministry have been open to the appointment of women. However, those ministries exclude the roles of pastor and elder.

**Churches of Christ** function as a non-denomination. They have no head of communion or organizational structure but instead function as a networked fellowship. Each church calls its own ministers by its own standards. The point of access is a local church and relationships with local pastors. Generally, the role of women is subordinate to men.[13]

**Church of God: Anderson, Indiana,** assists pastors in their search for churches via an online clergy site. The level of assistance to clergy and congregations varies by state assemblies. The churches have congregational autonomy, so they search and call. Clergy desiring to be considered by a Church of God should contact the state or regional organization. Church of God Anderson affirms the call and advancement of women as pastors and leaders in the local church.[14]

The **Church of the Nazarene** is the largest holiness denomination in the United States. Its placement process as described by Kenneth Crow and Charles Crow is also a hybrid. The district superintendent works with the local church board to understand and articulate what the church is looking for in a pastor. The superintendent arranges interviews until, as a result of theses interviews; the local church board identifies a candidate to recommend to the church for a vote. The congregational vote is the call issued by the local church.[15]

Candidates must become known and valued by district superintendents. The Crows describe the best-case scenario for candidates as those who "create a demand for their services." Building and maintaining relationships with denominational leaders is the coin of the realm. From the denomination's founding meeting, Nazarenes affirmed the ministry of women in "all offices of the church including ministry." Indeed, the founder, Phineas F. Bresee, often said, "Some of our best men are women."[16]

**Disciples of Christ** use a web-based ministerial profile system. The process uses a ministerial profile to communicate information about candidates. They also require disclosure forms and a clergy criminal background check. This process allows clergy to identify preferences for distribution of material.[17] A primary entry point would be the regional minister or area minister. Clergy standing within Disciples of Christ is granted and held by the geographic region in which one lives. Since the late nineteenth century, Disciples have ordained women to ministry. In 2002, about one fourth of Disciples clergy were women.

**Evangelical Covenant Church** utilizes the conference superintendent and/or the Department of the Ordered Ministry as the entry point for a minister open to a call. The covenant of orientation fulfills the requirements for ordination set by the Book of Ordered Ministry. The Evangelical Covenant Church does not place persons in local churches. Rather, it provides recommended names.[18] Churches are urged to interview only one candidate at a time. The local church is fully responsible for calling its ministers.[19]

The Evangelical Covenant Church affirms women in all ministry and leadership positions within the church, both lay and clergy. "We believe that the biblical basis for service in the body of Christ is giftedness, a call from God, and godly character—not gender."[20]

**Evangelical Free Church of America (EFCA)** uses an online process, Minister Connection.net. This data matching process is intended to help pastors and churches find each other. It is not a replacement for prayer and dependence on the Holy Spirit. Ministry Connection is now framed by Ask . . . Seek . . . Knock. Ask means asking questions of the exiting ministry, the desires of the congregation, and church health. The task of the search team is to Seek. They seek to codify a position description and identify a budget to guide their search. The Knock phase is evaluating and interviewing candidates, background checking, and ministry matching. This process considers leadership style, participation style, temperament, and ministry gifts and values.[21] The district superintendent serves as gatekeeper for persons wanting to be considered by EFCA churches. Women are affirmed in all positions other than senior pastor.

United Church of Christ (UCC) uses a search and call process that allows a local church to do a national search for its next clergy. This system provides similar support for UCC clergy who are seeking a call to service or to a new service. The process calls for completion of both a minister's profile and a congregational profile. Clergy and congregations work closely with a conference or association because those bodies facilitate the process. Clergy activate their process by subscribing to UCC Employment Opportunities, available from the UCC Office for Parish Life and Leadership. Everyone who participates in the process needs to submit to a complete background check. Clergy can fill out a clergy profile without subscribing to "Employment Opportunities," but then the process is not as effective.[22]

UCC has ordained women since the nineteenth century, and women are welcome as leaders at all levels of church life. The primary contacts for persons considering UCC ministry are conference and associational executives.[23]

Because the call process is held as an essential part of church life and relationship to the judicatories, it is necessary to be recognized or added to a pastoral registry before persons can become candidates. It will be necessary for interested persons to begin building a relationship with judicatories well in advance of being a candidate. Recognition by a specific judicatory may or may not give recognition in other judicatories. It will be necessary to clarify that issue in conversations.

## Connectional Denominations and Traditions

The **African Methodist Episcopal Church (AME)**, a historically black denomination, operates on a clergy appointment system. The process varies among the fourteen districts in the United States, but the entry point for the process is generally the senior pastor of the searching minister's home church. Contact information for specific districts is available on the denominational website.[24] The AME Church has long ordained women to pastoral ministry, and as is true of most connectional traditions, women clergy in the AME system have greater success finding placements in the local church than their free church sisters do.

The **Episcopal Church** search and call process revolves around ministry vacancies and clergy initiative. Congregations do a self-study and prepare a church profile. After completing these tasks, the congregation is ready to receive names. Clergy respond by submitting their material to the contact person in the local churches they are interested in. The congregations discern the strongest candidates. The diocese, through its deployment or transition officer, must provide approval from the bishop for individuals to be considered for a call to a specific congregation. The church is the calling and employing entity. Persons interested in serving an Episcopal congregation should consider it is the bishop who must approve a candidate before the call is issued and usually approves and checks the final slate of two or three candidates, interviewing them and checking with counterparts in the dioceses in which the candidate has previously served. The denomination's Office of Transition Ministry keeps a database of profiles for clergy and congregations, as well as offering a variety of resources for searching ministers.[25]

To be called as rector of a parish or vicar or priest in charge of a mission congregation, the person must be an ordained priest (or a transitional deacon about to be ordained priest) in good standing in the Episcopal Church. The only exception at this time is with the Evangelical Lutheran Church in America (ELCA), with whom the Episcopal Church shares a covenant, "Call to Common Mission," which allows some crossover with the bishop's and congregation's approval. The Episcopal Church has affirmed women in ordained ministry since 1976, although a few dioceses resisted this inclusiveness as late as this writing. The first female Episcopal bishop was consecrated in 1990, and in 2006, the denomination made history by elected a woman as presiding bishop.

The **Mennonite Church USA** has as a goal of its ministry transitions process to discern whether a congregation and a pastoral candidate have sufficiently common expectations, commitment, values, and beliefs so that a meaningful relationship can be established and covenants with each other can be made. Ministry transitions call for the candidates to complete a Ministerial Leadership Information (MLI) form and identification of pastoral expectations and skills. The potential candidates provide skill information in "Twenty Pastoral Areas." The conference offers guidance in the area of current salary, benefits, and reimbursement guidelines.

The conference minister provides the church a list of candidates, which includes brief biographical information. The conference or district holds the credentials for ministers, so that is the entry point for persons desiring to be considered in the Mennonite family.[26] It appears the relationship between congregations and clergy is covenant rather than call.

Women serve in the Mennonite family. An article in *The Mennonite* (April 2008) indicates women have closed the gap and now take no longer than men in securing their second placement.[27]

**The Reformed Church in America (RCA)** assigns responsibility for recognition of ministerial status to a classis, which is a local geographic organization. This body is guided by specific standards of the Reformed Church in America. Candidates must affirm understanding of and adherence to these standards.[28] The consistory (the local church board) is responsible for providing ministers for its church. This board will seek to learn the mind of the congregation with respect to a person who may be called to ministry in that church. The search itself is handled by a congregational search committee in most cases, as tasked by the consistory. The entry point for recognition is the classis, but in many instances, the local church may act independently.

Affirmation of women in ministry is emerging at various levels within the denomination, including the Leadership Development department's Call Waiting program for men and woman who sense a new call to ministry.[29] The program offers a variety of resources about the nature of ministry in the denomination and the preparation involved in pursuing a call. On the Ministry Services webpage, ministers and congregations can find information related to ministry transition (ministry opportunities listing, pastoral search manual, etc.).[30]

The **Evangelical Lutheran Church in America (ELCA)** also has a process in which the bishop or the bishop's representative plays a defining role. The local church council forms a call committee. This committee fills out the Ministry Site Profile, which guides the bishop's office in recruiting pastors to interview with the call committee. The bishop's office will nominate one to three candidates who are willing to be interviewed. Both the candidate and the church must agree for the process to proceed. The call committee recommends a candidate to the church council, and if the council concurs, it recommends the candidate to the church. Before the congregation holds a vote, the call committee and church council meet with the bishop's office to establish a salary and benefit package for the terms of call agreement. The local congregation then votes to extend a call to the candidate.[31]

Some dioceses have moved into much more of a coaching role with both congregations and candidates. The congregations have taken much more ownership in the process, as it truly is up to them and the Holy Spirit to discern the best-rostered leader for the congregation. Leaders may have their papers in more than one congregation at a time as well. The ELCA affirms women in all offices of the church, including ordination to pastoral ministry.

In **Presbyterian Churches USA (PCUSA)**, the presbytery has the primary responsibility for oversight of the call process. Presbyterians believe that pastors and congregations are brought together through a call from God. This call is confirmed by each of the members in a three-way partnership saying yes to the relationship. The partners are the presbytery, the local congregation, and the candidate. Women as well as men are affirmed and called in ordained ministry. The PCUSA process is centered on writing and submitting the church information to the presbytery. The presbytery then provides Personal Information Forms (a résumé) to the pastor nominating committee. After reference checks, personal interviews, and prayerful consideration, a nominee is presented to the congregation for election as pastor.[32]

The **United Methodist Church (UMC)** practices annual appointment of clergy. United Methodist clergy are members of annual conferences and not local churches. They are employees of the conference, not the local church. The average appointment lasts about four years, although there is no limit on how long clergy persons can serve the same church. It is unique in the United Methodist system that each local church is ensured a pastor, and all ordained clergy in good standing will receive appointment.[33] The primary entrance point for United Methodist churches is the district superintendent of a conference. Women are called and appointed at all levels of denominational leadership and service in the UMC, including appointments as senior pastors and bishops.

The **Church of God in Christ (COGIC)** is a historical black denomination in the holiness tradition. Its polity is episcopal, with each jurisdiction governed by a bishop under the larger oversight of the General Assembly and General Board (Presidium). No information about clergy appointments or the search and call process was found on the denominational website or related resources, so it is recommended that ministers in this tradition contact their local church pastor or the bishop of their home jurisdiction to learn more about the entry point for application and consideration.[34] Women in the COGIC who experience a call to ministry may be licensed as missionaries (deaconess missionaries or evangelist missionaries, but they may not be ordained to the offices of elder, pastor, or bishop.[35]

NOTES

1. http://www.abhms.org/abps/ (accessed March 29, 2011).

2. http://www.convergeworldwide.org/mobilize-churches/church-staffing (accessed March 29, 2011).

3. http://thefellowship.info/About-Us/What-We-Do/Reference-and-Referral (accessed March 29, 2011).

4. http://www.thefellowship.info/About-Us/FAQ (accessed March 10, 2010).

5. http://www.sbc.net/aboutus/pswomen.asp (accessed March 29, 2011).

6. http://nationalbaptist.com/index.php?nid=146811&s=rs (accessed March 25, 2011).

7. http://www.pnbc.org/PNBC/Home.html (accessed March 25, 2011).

8. Constitution of the General Council of the Assemblies of God, revised August 8–11, 2007, Indianapolis, Indiana.

9. http://www.brethren.org/site/DocServer/12MinisterialRelationships .pfd?docID=172 (accessed March 29, 2011).

10. http://www.brethren.org/site/DocServer/1999_Women_in_Ministry .pdf?docID=861 (accessed March 29, 2011).

11. http://www.cmalliance.org/serve/senior-pastor (accessed March 29, 2011).

12. http://www.cmalliance.org/serve/transfer.jsp (accessed March 29, 2011).

13. http://church-of-christ.org/ (accessed March 29, 2011).

14. http://www.chog.org/Ministries/WomeninMinistry/tabid/413/Default .aspx (accessed March 29, 2011).

15. Kenneth E. Crow and Charles D. Crow, "Dynamics of the Placement Process," (paper presented at Association of Nazarene Sociologists and Researchers, March 13–15, 2003) 10.

16. Quoted in Carmen Renee Barry, *The Unauthorized Guide to Choosing a Church* (Grand Rapids: Brazos Press, 2003), 291.

17. http://www.discipleshomemissions.org/pages/CV-Search_Call (accessed March 29, 2011).

18. http://www.covchurch.org/ministry/ministerial-call-process (accessed March 29, 2011).

19. *The Calling of a New Pastor: A Guide for the Pastoral Search Committees* (Chicago: The Central Conference of the Evangelical Covenant Church, 1995), 4.

20. Sharon Cairns Mann, *Called and Gifted* (Chicago: Covenant Publications, 2005), 2. http://www.covchurch.org/resources/files/2010/04/Called-and-Gifted-booklet-2.10.pdf (accessed March 29, 2011).

21. http://www.efca.org/church-health/pastoral-care-staff-benefits/ministerconnection-placement-service (accessed March 29, 2011).

22. http://www.ucc.org/ministers/profile/ (accessed March 29, 2011).

23. http://www.accsd.org/UCC.html (accessed March 29, 2011).

24. This information was provided by the denomination's current General Secretary, Dr. Clement W. Fugh. See http://www.ame-church.com/directory/presiding-bishops.php for more information, including contact information for judicatory leadership.

25. http://www.episcopalchurch.org/109541_ENG_HTM.htm (accessed March 29, 2011).

26. http://www.mennoniteusa.org/Default.aspx?tabid=235 (accessed March 29, 2011).

27. Anna Groff, "Women in Ministry Trajectories Continue," *The Mennonite* (April 15, 2008), 20. http://www.themennonite.org/issues/11-8/articles/Women_in_ministry_trajectories_continue# (accessed March 29, 2011).

28. *The Book of Church Order* (New York: Reformed Church Press, 2009), 1, 48, 49.

29. https://www.rca.org/sslpage.aspx?pid=2024 (accessed March 29, 2011).

30. https://www.rca.org/sslpage.aspx?pid=1907 (accessed March 29, 2011).

31. "Call Process for Calling a Pastor," La Crosse Area Synod, ELCA, June 4, 2009, 1-4,
http://www.lacrosseareasynod.org/wp-content/uploads/callpstr.pdf (accessed March 29, 2011).

32. "On Calling a Pastor," Church Leadership Connection, Office of Vocation, Presbyterian Church (U.S.A.), 8, 10.
www.pcusa.org/media/uploads/clc/pdfs/callingpastor.pdf (accessed March 29, 2011).

33. http://archives.umc.org/interior.asp?ptid=1&mid=3701 (accessed March 29, 2011).

34. http://cogic.net (accessed March 25, 2011).

35. http://en.wikipedia.org/wiki/Church_of_God_in_Christ (accessed March 25, 2011).

# Resource for Evaluation

This material in this appendix was gleaned from information received sometime around 1998 and reflects the process of evaluation in the United Methodist Church. The resource listed twelve functions of ministry and nine personal qualities of ordained ministry.

## Twelve Functions of Ministry

**1.** Our pastor's/my **preaching ministry** . . . uses sound biblical content? Uses sound theological content? Sermons move toward a goal? Is there thorough preparation? Makes effective use of voice, gestures, mannerisms, facial expression, and eye contact? Is relevant to personal needs, social/justice issues, and spiritual growth? Is challenging, motivating, inspiring, comforting, and informative?

**2.** Our pastor's/my **teaching ministry** . . . uses a variety of learning methods with children, youth, and adults? In a teaching event diagnoses learning needs and sets learning goals? Adjusts a teaching opportunity to the appropriate age level characteristics? Presents Christian concepts to children, youth, and adults? Provides learning opportunities for varied groups of youth? Uses the sermon and worship services as opportunities for teaching? Uses planning/administrative meetings as teaching opportunities? Does leadership training?

**3.** Our pastor's/our church's/my **worship leading** . . . plans service as an integral unit? Uses music that fits the theme of the service? Conducts worship with confidence and dignity? Provides an atmosphere of expectancy? Is open to experimentation? Uses a variety of resources, both traditional and contemporary? Encourages a sense of community? Raises awareness of human needs? Provides meaningful time of prayer? Uses a good selection of Bible resources? Administers the sacraments, weddings, and funerals meaningfully?

**4.** Our pastor's/our church's/my leadership in the **connectional ministry** of [insert name of your denomination here] . . . is knowledgeable about the denomination's programs and persuasive in promoting them? Is able to interpret and tailor the denominations resources for the local church? Creates a climate of enthusiasm and understanding for the denomination? Participates in the denominational events at all levels? Challenges the congregation to be involved in the wider mission of the church?

**5.** Our pastor's/our church's/my leadership in **evangelism** . . . is effective in one-to-one witnessing? Equips others to witness? Provides for assimilation of new members? Effectively visits new residents? Preaches for commitment? Effectively leads membership and baptism classes?

**6.** Our pastor's/our church's/my leadership in **educational ministries** . . . is effective at goal setting? Is supportive of teachers and officers? Trains and supports teachers and officers? Trains and supervises teachers? Participates in planning and evaluating the church school? Knows and supports denominational resources? Effectively promotes the program and growth of the church school? Enables ministry for children and youth? Is open to experimentation and innovation? Provides theological reflection and faith development for teachers?

**7.** Our pastor's/our church's/my **pastoral care ministry** . . . is helping persons grow in their relationship to God in times of crisis? Is acquainted with parish families and their needs? Expresses care and support? Counseling needs are assessed and referred to appropriate providers? Is skilled at listening sensitively? Responds immediately to needs? Offers comfort and healing? Communicates supportive love? Enables awareness of God's presence?

**8.** Our pastor's/our church's/my **visitation ministries** . . . visits are made for the purpose of listening, representing, promoting, problem solving? Visits are made with the sick and shut-in for spiritual direction, to communicate a sense of belonging, and to provide a supportive presence? Visits are regularly made to the congregation? Follow-up is made of initial contacts?

**9.** Our pastor's/our church's/my leadership in **community ministries** . . . understands community needs? Participates in community organizations, events, and ecumenical agencies? Provides care for persons outside the church? Has theological foundation for community involvement? Is skilled in working with community organizations and issues? Is sensitive to the poor, suffering, and disadvantaged? Accepts community leadership?

**10.** Our pastor's/our church's/my leadership in **ecumenical ministries** . . . encourages ecumenical cooperation? Is knowledgeable of faith and practices of other faiths and religions? Represents and interprets [denominational faith group] theology and practices to others? Interprets objectively the attitudes and positions of other denominations? Informs the church of ecumenical issues? Participates in ecumenical programs? Leads congregation to be involved with other congregations?

**11.** Our pastor's/my leadership of this **congregation's ministry** . . . helps groups to diagnose needs, establish goals, develop strategies and plans, reflect theologically on goals and style, make decisions, and evaluate results? Is effective at conflict utilization and resolution? Builds a team with good interpersonal relations? Is an imaginative problem solver? Knows external conditions facing the church? Holds self and others accountable for ministry? Leads administrative committees to reflect theologically on their goals, policies, and programs? Promotes and creates enthusiasm for church programs?

**12.** Our pastor's/my **administration** of the congregation's ministries . . . attends to details? Is responsible in answering messages and mail? Provides clear, organized agendas? Uses time effectively?

Effectively delegates task? Provides clear direction for others? Keeps adequate and neat records? Is punctual and attentive to appointments? Effectively communicates? Utilizes skill and time of others volunteer and paid?

## Nine Personal Qualities

The evaluation also lists and asks questions about nine personal qualities of ordained ministers:

- Relates to persons
- Is self-aware
- Possesses integrity and acts with self-control
- Is open to growth and learning
- Is loyal to the call to ministry and the mission of the church
- Is organized and intentional
- Has energy, health, and enthusiasm
- Exhibits a growing personal faith
- Has a leadership style that enables and supports the participation and work of others